BLACK LAWS
OF VIRGINIA

A SUMMARY OF THE LEGISLATIVE ACTS OF VIRGINIA
CONCERNING NEGROES FROM EARLIEST
TIMES TO THE PRESENT

BY

June Purcell Guild, LL.M.

COMPILED BY KAREN HUGHES WHITE AND JOAN PETERS
AFRO-AMERICAN HISTORICAL ASSOCIATION
OF FAUQUIER COUNTY, VIRGINIA
1996

HERITAGE BOOKS
2011

HERITAGE BOOKS

AN IMPRINT OF HERITAGE BOOKS, INC.

Books, CDs, and more—Worldwide

For our listing of thousands of titles see our website
at
www.HeritageBooks.com

A Facsimile Reprint
Published 2011 by
HERITAGE BOOKS, INC.
Publishing Division
100 Railroad Ave. #104
Westminster, Maryland 21157

— Publisher's Notice —
In reprints such as this, it is often not possible to remove blemishes from the
original. We feel the contents of this book warrant its reissue despite these
blemishes and hope you will agree and read it with pleasure.

International Standard Book Numbers
Paperbound: 978-1-888265-19-4
Clothbound: 978-0-7884-8883-2

FORWARD TO 1995 EDITION OF JUNE GUILD'S
BLACK LAWS OF VIRGINIA: NOTES FROM THE EDITORS

Karen Hughes White is an experienced family historian and speaker about topics concerning African-American history and genealogy. She is the co-founder of the Afro-American Historical Association of Fauquier County and a co-author of <u>Fauquier County Virginia Registers of Free Negroes</u>.

Joan Peters is a local historian, genealogist, lecturer, and author. She is currently serving as the historian for the Afro-American Historical Association of Fauquier County, Virginia and is the author of <u>Local Records and Genealogy: A Primer for the Family Historian</u> and <u>Local Sources for African-American Family Historians</u>.

On behalf of the Afro-American Historical Association of Fauquier County, Virginia, we are very pleased to present a reproduction of June Guild's original 1936 edition of <u>Black Laws of Virginia</u> to the research public. We have left the original edition as it was, adding only a new title page, forward and introduction to this 1995 edition

One of A.A.H.A.'s goals is to present new editions of out-of-print books dealing with African-American history and genealogy. June Guild's classic treatment of the laws that affected the Negro in Virginia will, we hope, serve as the centerpiece of our efforts.

June Guild's <u>Black Laws</u> illustrates how important it is for researchers to have a knowledge of the law when they are doing African-American history or genealogy. These laws permeated the life of the eighteenth and nineteenth century Negro, whether slave or free; and by implication, the fabric of life for the white majority.

It is the law that bound the two races together and it is the law that portrayed the harsh and restricted conditions under which African-American, bond and free, lived. In many ways, the response is a testament to African-American resilience, dignity and perseverance.

Karen White
Joan Peters
Warrenton, Virginia
Spring, 1995

Introduction to the 1995 Edition of June Guild's Black Laws of Virginia

By Joan W. Peters,
Historian of A.A.H.A. of Fauquier County

1. Introduction

Both Virginia's colonial legislature and the state's General Assembly passed a massive amount of legislation relating to slaves and the free Negro. The laws that resulted were left to the local jurisdictions to interpret and enforce. In this instance, this was the local county court system.

2. Virginia and the Negro in the Seventeenth Century

Negroes first appeared in Virginia in August 1619, transported aboard a Dutch frigate, not as slaves but as indentured servants. These twenty Negroes, three of whom were women, bound themselves as indentured servants, to work for masters for a specified length of time in return for their passage across the Atlantic. For the next seventy-five years, indentured servitude by both Negroes and whites provided a satisfactory solution to the need for a labor supply.

By 1691, this situation had undergone a dramatic change and it became customary to hold black indentured servants past their term of service. A variety of factors contributed to this change in status for black indentured servants. The supply of free labor decreased while their costs went up. Britain began to take control of the lucrative African and Caribbean slave trade so that there were larger numbers of Negroes from those countries for export to America. By the mid 1660s, Virginia law recognized the word "slave" as referring to an existing class, thus creating a legal basis for slavery. At the same time, the small yeoman holdings were superseded by plantations, dependent upon crops like tobacco and strategically situated along the major rivers leading to the Atlantic. This in turn led to a greater demand for an agricultural labor force.

In 1662, the colonial legislature enacted a law stating that the children of Englishmen and Negro women were to be slave or free according to the condition of the mother.

In 1680, the tidewater planters, now in control of the legislature, were worried enough about the meetings held by their black bondsmen at plantation gatherings and at burials to usher passage of a law forbidding arms such as clubs, staffs, guns, swords or other weapons to Negroes and slaves; furthermore, slaves were forbidden to leave their owner's plantation without a certificate and then only when necessary.

In 1681, the legislature became alarmed at the "inconvenience" to the colony that occurred upon the emancipation of Negroes and mulattos (and its resultant increase in a free Negro population). They feared that these freed slaves might entice other Negroes from their master's service, or become recipients of stolen goods, or be so elderly that the county would have to maintain them. So the legislature passed a law forbidding emancipation of any Negro or mulatto unless the owner paid for his transportation outside Virginia within six months of setting the slave free. This law had the effect of making black bondsmen slaves for life.

In the same year, the legislature passed the first of many laws outlawing intermarriage between an English or other white man or woman, bond or free, to a Negro, mulatto, or Indian man or woman, bond or free. The penalty was banishment from Virginia.

In 1696, the colonial legislature reiterated that the condition of children born in Virginia, whether bond or free, was according to the condition of the mother. IF the mother was a free woman of color, the child was free. If the mother was a slave, the child was also a slave.

3. A Sampling of Virginia's laws relating to slaves and free Negroes before the Revolutionary War

- **Emancipation**

In 1705, alarmed by the numbers of free Negroes who owned slaves, the legislature decreed that no Negro, mulatto, or Indian could purchase any Christian servant, except of their own complexion, as slaves. Negroes were forbidden to purchase any white Christian servant. During the same year, they reaffirmed the restrictions in travel, forbidding slaves to lave the plantation on which they lived without a certificate of leave. Slaves were also forbidden weapons. Penalties for disobeying this law was twenty lashes for either offense.

In 1723, the legislature addressed emancipation once more. Negro and indian slaves could not be set free except for meritorious service which was to be so adjudged by the Governor and Council. If slaves were freed without the approval of the Governor and Council, the parish Churchwardens were to sell the emancipated slave at public auction. The proceeds were then to be applied for the use of the parish. This law was to remain in effect until after the American Revolution.

- **Slaves as property**

The colonial legislature addressed the nature of slavery as property twice during the eighteenth century. Earlier in the century, in 1705, they decided that Negroes, mulattos, and indian slaves held within Virginia, were to be held as real estate and not chattel and could descend unto heirs and widows according to the custom of land inheritance. Slaves, whether Negro, mulatto, or indian, could be help in absolute ownership. In 1748, this law was repealed and replace with an ordinance stating that Negroes, mulattos and indian slaves were to be considered personal property.

- **Voting Rights**

The colonial legislature moved to abolish voting rights for free Negroes and Indians in 1723.

4. Eighteenth century laws regarding illegitimate children and poor orphans and poor children of color

There were several laws passed during the eighteenth century regarding illegitimate children and poor orphans or poor children of color. In 1705, indentured women servants who had illegitimate children by a Negro or mulatto, were liable for a L15 fine for the use of the parish or sale of the servant for five years after the expiration of her original indenture. The children of such a union were to be bound out as servants until they reached the age of thirty-one.

Sixty years later, in 1765, the legislature passed a law decreeing that illegitimate children of women servants and Negroes or free Christian white women by Negroes, were to be bound out. The boys were to serve until they reached the age of twenty-one, the girls until they were eighteen.

In 1785, the General Assembly transferred this responsibility to the Overseers of the Poor. Then, in the first decade of the nineteenth century, Overseers of the Poor were forbidden to bind out any black or mulatto orphan to a master that would teach his apprentice reading, writing, or arithmetic.

5. Sheep Farming and Black Laws

In 1752, the legislature moved to protect sheep farming. This law prohibited Negroes or slaves from carrying any dog whatsoever from one plantation to another. The penalty for ignoring the law was two fold: the death of the dog and a whipping of 20 lashes on the perpetrator. There was, however, nothing in this law to hinder an owner from sending his slave from place to place with the owner's hounds, spaniels, pointers or setters.

6. Black Laws After the Revolutionary War

- **Emancipation**

The last two decades of the eighteenth century saw the General Assembly pass a host of laws relating to free Negroes and to slaves. Following the aftermath of the American Revolution and its ideals engendered by the Declaration of Independence, the Virginia legislature decided to allow emancipation of slaves by deed, will, or other instrument of writing. The document had to be signed, sealed and witnessed.

The former owner was to be responsible for the support of any emancipated slaves not of sound mind and body or over the age of forty-five. Likewise, the emancipator was to be responsible for children— boys under 21 years of age and girls under 18 years of age. A copy of the emancipation was to be given to the freed slave. The penalty for being with a copy was jail, especially if the freed slave traveled outside the county. Liberated slaves, who could not pay parish or county levies, could be hired out by the Sheriff for as long as it took to raise the taxes they owed.

During this same period, the General Assembly granted immediate emancipation to any Negro slave who had served in the Revolutionary war. For owners neglecting to emancipate these veterans, the General Assembly gave them the right to petition the local County Court for the right to sue for their freedom.

- Legal definitions

Two years after the close of the Revolutionary War, the members of the Virginia General Assembly wrestled with the definitions of Negro and mulatto. Every person whose grandfathers of grandmothers were Negro, although all other progenitors were white, were to be deemed as "Negro". Any person with one quarter or more Negro blood was to be deemed "mulatto."

- Restrictions to individual rights

At the same time that the Assembly was loosening some of the bonds of slavery, they were tightening others. In 1785, the General Assembly enacted legislation prescribing slaves from traveling from his residence without a license or a letter showing he has permission to do so from his master. Slaves were also forbidden to keep arms; riots and unlawful assemblies were punishable by whipping.

The year 1792 was a busy year for law makers and for legislation relating to free Negroes. In that year, Negroes and mulattos were forbidden to carry firearms although free Negroes could be permitted one gun; Negroes, bond or free, living on the frontier could be licensed to carry a gun. In 1806, free Negroes were prescribed from carrying a "firelock" of any kind without a license.

In 1792, there were a variety of other laws passed: conspiracy to rebel, or make or cause an insurrection, became a felony punishable by death. Negro and mulatto slaves were adjudged to be personal estate. Slaves were not to trade as free men. Intermarriage between a Negro man or woman and a free white man or woman was punishable by a six month jail term. The legislature levied a $30.00 fine on the parties involved and a $250.00 fine on the minister.

- Certificates of Freedom

Other laws were passed that related to indentured servants who were issued a Certificate of Freedom upon satisfactory proof of the termination of their service. The county courts extended this certificate to emancipated Negroes upon proof of their emancipation by deed or will or other instrument of writing.

- **Apprenticeships and Care of the Poor**

In 1765, the colonial legislature passed legislation dealing with apprentice-ships. The House of Burgesses provided apprenticeships for bastard children of women servants and Negroes or free white women by Negroes. Boys were to be "bound out" until they were twenty-one; girls until they were eighteen. The former law apprenticing children until they were thirty-one was thought to be to severe on the children and repealed.

In 1785, legislation provided for district overseers of the poor in each county. The Assembly transferred powers held by the old churchwarden system to the overseers of the poor.

Then, in 1792, the General Assembly passed a law providing for the poor, lame, blind and others who are unable to maintain themselves. They empowered overseers of the poor to provide poor houses, nurses and doctors for the care of the poor.

The county courts directed the overseers of the poor to apprentice poor orphans and children to a person that the court approved. Boys were bound out until they were twenty-one, girls until they were eighteen.

- **The "Quasi-free": the practice of hiring slaves out as free**

The year 1793 proved to be as busy. The legislature voted to stop the practice of Negro slaves from hiring out as free persons and to keep a closer eye on the free Negro populations found through out the local communities in the Commonwealth.

Slave holders had tended to allow their Negro slaves to hire themselves out, especially those who were skilled artisans. Now, the legislature forbade this practice; owners of these "quasi-free" slaves could be indicted by a grand jury for hiring their slaves out contrary to law; the Negro slave found himself in jail while the owner was hauled into court and made to pay jail fees.

- **Registers of Free Negroes**

During the same year, the General Assembly passed legislation to register all free Negroes and mulattos in the Commonwealth with the clerk of the Court in the community in which they lived. who were free to sell their services, were to be registered and numbered in a book kept by the town Clerk. This register recorded name, age, color, status and emancipation details--by whom and in which county court the registrant had been freed.

The law required free Negroes and mulattos to re-register every three years. Unregistered free Negroes could be jailed as runaway slaves.

These certificates and registers served as the free Negroes' legal identity; these "free papers" as they came to be called, kept free people of color from jail or from being identified mistakenly as slaves. Recent research indicates that while some free Negroes came in to make the initial registration, many did not re-register unless their original papers had been lost.

Laws involving the registration of free Negroes remained in effect until the Civil War. Only one substantial change was made and that occurred in 1834. The Court alone could order the registration of free Negroes by the clerk of the county court. the register was now to include notes of marks and scars in the description of the registrant.

- **Law for Petitions to sue for Freedom**

The General Assembly also made it lawful in 1793 for any Negro slave who felt that he or she was held illegally in bondage to petition the Court for the right to sue for their freedom. Research concerning these petitions suggest that while there were some notices of these suits in local county courts, there were only a few instances in the Minutes or Orders where one could trace the outcome of these petitions.

Laws about forging counterfeit registers

In 1795, the legislature decreed that any person who forged or counterfeited papers giving a slave freedom was to pay a $200.00 fine and suffer imprisonment for one year without bail.

8. A Sampling of Nineteenth Century Black Law

- ### Commissioner of Revenue Lists of Free Negroes

In 1801, the state legislature decreed that county commissioners of revenue were to return a complete list of all free Negroes in their districts on an annual basis. This list was to contain names, gender, residence and trade of each free Negro. A copy of the list was to be posted on the door of the county court house. If a registered free Negro moved to another county, then magistrates there could issue a warrant for him, unless he was employed. Otherwise, he would be jailed as a vagrant.

- ### Petitions to remain in Virginia

In 1806, the General Assembly moved to remove the free Negro population from Virginia with a law that stated that all emancipated slaves, freed after May 1, 1806, who remained in the Commonwealth for more than a year, would forfeit his right to freedom and be sold by the Overseers of the Poor for the benefit of the parish. Families wishing to stay were to petition the legislature through the local county court.

In 1826 the Sheriff replaced the Overseers of the Poor as the selling agent for free Negroes remaining in Virginia. The Court could authorize this sale only upon a jury verdict or confession by the party. In 1831 this law was amended slightly: the sheriff could sell the free Negroes at public auction who remained in Virginia contrary to the 1806 law.

This law remained in effect until 1837 when the General Assembly changed their mind, inundated by this time with petitions from free Negroes and from whites dependent upon their skills. Now, the legislature said, any slave emancipated since May 1, 1806 could apply to the local court for permission to remain in Virginia.

Upon satisfactory proof that the petitioner was of good character, peaceable, orderly, industrious, and not addicted to drunkenness, gaming or other vices, permission could be granted. A notice had to appear on the court house door for two months announcing the petitioner's intention to remain in the State and three quarters of the justices of the court had to agree that the individual, couple, or family could remain.

- **Asylum for freed slaves outside the continental United States**

In 1816, the General Assembly sought to obtain asylum beyond the United States for free persons of color and passed a resolution to request the Governor to correspond to the President for the purpose of obtaining territory on the coast of Africa, or on the shore of the North Pacific, now within the boundaries of the United States, which would serve as an asylum for free Negroes.

Then in 1833, after the abortive Nat Turner slave rebellion, the legislature appropriated $18,000.00 per year for five years to encourage the transportation and subsistence of free persons of color to emigrate to Liberia or other areas on the west coast of Africa.

- **Criminal Offenses**

In 1823, any free Negro who was convicted of an offense punishable by imprisonment for more than two years, was now punished by whipping and sold as a slave and banished from Virginia, at the discretion of the Court or a jury. If free Negroes or slaves willfully assaulted and beat a white person with intent to killed and was convicted of this offense, they too could be punished by a public whipping and banishment from the state. If the convicted person returned to Virginia, he or she could be hung.

- **Impact of Nat Turner's failed slave rebellion**

After the failure of the Nat Turner slave rebellion in 1830, the Virginia General Assembly passed a variety of laws curtailing slave and free Negroes' right to assembly. To prevent free Negroes from assembling and speaking at church, the legislature forbade preaching by slaves, free Negroes or mulattos at religious meetings. Indeed free people of color and slaves were forbidden to hold any religious meeting during the day or evening. The penalty for violating this ordinance was a public whipping of thirty-nine lashes.

Slaves attending religious meetings without the consent of their master were also liable to a public whipping. However, religious instruction to slaves of free Negroes could be given during the day by a licensed white minister and the slaves of any one owner could assemble for religious instruction during the day.

In 1832, the Assembly addressed riots, unlawful assembly, trespass, sedition, and conspiracy to commit insurrection. If slaves or free Negroes wrote or printed anything advising people of color to commit insurrectior or rebellion, the perpetrators were to be whipped. The same penalty was instituted for riots, unlawful assembly, trespass and seditious speeches.

During the same year, the legislature prohibited Negroes from selling or giving away liquor near any public assembly. The penalty for violating this law was also a public whipping.

- **Free Negroes' rights to own slaves**

Another law passed in 1832 curtailed the rights of free people of color to own slaves. After this date, no free Negro would be able to acquire ownership of any slave, except through inheritance, other than his or her spouse or children.

In 1858, further restrictions took place. Free Negroes could now own slaves only through inheritance.

- **Laws that curtailed individual rights**

In 1843, the legislature curtailed slave and free Negro rights to dispense medicine. Selling, preparing or administering medicine became a misdemeanor whose penalty was a public whipping. Preparations of drugs by free Negroes that caused abortions carried a penalty of five to ten years in prison. If slave prepared a drug to cause abortion, the first time offender received a public whipping. Any offense after that was a hanging offense.

In 1858 free people of color could not buy wine or ardent spirits unless they had written permission from three or more justices that they were sober, orderly and of good character. In 1860, free Negroes could not be ordinary or tavern keepers and were prescribed from selling hard liquor.

- Laws relating to Criminal Offenses

In 1846, the General Assembly granted justices of the peace the right to try any free Negro who committed simple larceny or offenses valued to $20.00. If convicted, the free Negro faced a public whipping of thirty-nine lashes. If acquitted, the acquittal was final.

If a free person of color assaulted a white person with intent to kill, his conviction carried with it a prison term between five and eighteen years.

In 1860, the legislature decreed that free Negroes who committed offenses punishable by imprisonment in the penitentiary could be, at the discretion of the county court, sold into absolute slavery.

The foregoing is a sampling of the laws passed by the Virginia legislature before the Civil War. It is against this back drop of legislation that the editors invite your inspection of June Guild's enduring classic: the <u>Black Laws of Virginia.</u>

Contents

Contents *(Continued)*

INTRODUCTION

TEN PER CENT of Americans are Negroes; of Virginians, twenty-seven per cent are Negroes. That a national menace may lurk in the unfavorable status of such a large group seems to be dimly realized at last. There is even a growing consciousness that after all Negroes are human beings and American citizens to whom a Christian Democracy may owe fair treatment.

Today as never before, white Americans are wanting to know: Why are Negro tuberculosis and death rates universally high when Negro birth rates indicate great fertility and vigor, when some Negroes live to extreme old age and others are outstanding examples of physical development and stamina? Why do the whites of a community always make a poor showing in all social statistics when the Negroes make a poor showing? What is the correlation between high Negro illegitimacy and crime rates, and bad housing and poor schools, especially in the Black South? What will be the final outcome of those Southern subterfuges whereby Negroes are denied political and civil rights, and equal educational opportunities? Do untrained, unemployed, and unemployable Blacks tend to become Reds? Do Negroes absorb themselves in routine religion or participate in silly and dangerous religious sects because other forms of recreation are largely denied them, or merely because they once had to steal away to Jesus? Is race amalgamation the only answer to America's race question?

Negroes, too, even in the Black South, are beginning to take accurate inventory of their race difficulties and race progress. More and more often they are asking themselves and interested whites: Why are we discriminated against in every division of life? When and how will our political and economic deliverance come? Where is the justice in blaming us for conditions made for us and not by us?

In an effort to answer such questions as these courses in race relations, social legislation, and crime are offered in colleges and schools of social work, inter-racial committees and conferences meet, studies and surveys of race problems are made, churches conduct inter-racial services, books and magazine articles dealing with the various issues are published. But obviously the present and future of the Negro in the United States cannot be comprehended without a better understanding of his past. Negroes are among the authentic first families of Virginia, having been admitted here over three hundred and seventeen years ago. What has happened to them here may be taken as a rough measure of what has happened to them in the South where the majority of them continue to live.

This book deals exclusively with the status of the Virginia Negro, bond and free, as tracted through the laws, resolutions[1] and ordinances of the Virginia Assembly beginning with the earliest records and coming down to the present, with the addition of a few pertinent sections from Virginia constitutions. Law always reflects the social condition and thinking of the people who make it. This summary of the major enactments of the Virginia Assembly, therefore, not only clarifies the legal position of the Negro but reveals something of the official attitude of the people with whom his fate was—and is—cast. At the same time it indicates the historical beginnings of many of the disadvantages and discriminations surrounding him today as well as deeply embedded causes for his own racial attitudes and customs. It is the hope of

[1]Resolutions are no longer included in the official printed session laws but lack the historical interest of slavery days, but see page 99, note.

the writer that white Americans, including Virginians, reading this book and noting harshness has solved no human problems in the past will decide to grant Negroes of tomorrow fairer political, economic, and educational opportunities. Negroes should gain a better understanding of their own problems by a perusal of these pages and, perhaps, derive moderate courage from seeing the improvements which three hundred years, even seventy years, have brought them.

This compilation, then, is an effort to digest Virginia legislation on Negroes and arrange it chronologically by years under appropriate chapter headings. Several difficulties were encountered in the undertaking, including lack of uniformity and accuracy in legal terminology and principles, poor printing and indexing, the peculiar English, spelling, and numbering in the original laws. Also, in the first place, although human slavery is at least as old as Joseph and his brethren and has been practiced by Grecians, Romans, Africans and Englishmen alike the first Negroes landed in Virginia came without previous agreement or legal arrangement. In the beginning there was no law or custom to define the status of a Negro in the colony; Virginia law on the subject had to be developed and consequently frequently amended. Slavery, of course, was practiced in Anglo Saxon England and after the Conquest was replaced by feudal serfdom or villeinage. But the power of the medieval church, except in reference to its own manorial holdings was usually against open, legalized human slavery. The Black Death in 1348, followed by the preaching of John Ball[2] and the Peasants' Revolt of 1381, rather effectually abolished English slavery in the technical, legal sense and substituted therefor a new kind of legal terminology, where, within legally fixed conditions there was so-called freedom of contract between master or employer

[2] Se Appendix II.

and servant or employee. After the Conquest, William attempted to abolish the slave trade out of Bristol, although Wilburforce in 1788 failed to secure the passage of a law again abolishing the trade. Actually this was not done until 1806; not until 1833 did Parliament pass an act abolishing slavery throughout the British colonies and providing for the compensation of those hitherto entitled to the services of slaves. While therefor English attitudes, law, and practice on slavery have been by no means nobly consistent in an habeas corpus proceeding in 1772, Lord Mansfield held a Virginia slave in England became free as there was no English law to support slavery. Mansfield said "the state of slavery is so odious that nothing can be suffered to support it but positive law. I cannot say this case is allowed or approved by the law of England and therefore the Black must be discharged.[3] However, the Virginia Assembly repeatedly enacted that a slave in England should not be discharged from slavery,[4] and proceeded over a long period of years to build up principles to govern its own institution.

Although Jamestown, then called James Cittie or Citty, was settled in 1607, the first Assembly did not convene until 1619; no laws on the subject of slavery were passed then or for many years afterward. By a curious twist of fate the Commonwealth of Massachusetts passed a law on slavery twenty years before the Commonwealth of Virginia took legal notice of slavery; Connecticut also antedated Virginia by eleven years in its slavery law. The remarkable ease with which Negroes accepted Christianity led to the passage of many Virginia laws. If a Negro were a Christian should he not be free? So to order would have been a disastrous financial policy for the struggling province. On the other hand, if color

[3]Somerset v. Stewart. Loffts' Reports.
[4]1705, XLIX; 1748, XIV; 1753, VII.

alone differentiated the black man from the indentured convict or other white servant who came to Virginia by contract actual or implied, what would the colony do with its free Negroes? Indians did not readily accept the Christian's creed and were generally unsubmissive. Accordingly, Indian slavery proved unprofitable and was not long lived in the state. This digest of laws includes material on these and many other points as developed in the General Assembly of Virginia from time to time, although the material on Indian slavery is given only as incidental to Negro slavery.

In that historic year, 1619, the Virginia Company shipped to the little outpost on the banks of the mud-colored James one hundred orphans as apprentices or indented servants. In 1620, the same year when a sturdy band of yoemen with no clamor of cavalier or gentleman also set sail for America, the Lord Mayor of London agreed to send another hundred street boys to Jamestown. In 1619 came the first hundred convicts banished to a life of servitude in the wild new country which needed tobacco hands and was shortly to need a few cotton pickers as well. There came also at this time the first consignment of maids seeking husbands. Indenture, based on contracting, apprenticing, "spiriting," and involuntary servitude were known in England at the time. Naturally, therefore, the indenture of servants and the institution of slavery became closely allied, legally and socially in Virginia; many of the early laws were enacted for the "better government of servants and slaves." Serving as indentured servants in Virginia were not only Negroes, orphan boys, convicts, workingmen, but some who might truthfully be described as gentlemen. There is nothing to indicate that the position of the Negro was conspicuously different or less comfortable than the lot of most of the others at first. Many of the citations on servants and slaves, in the sixteen hundreds especially, indicate clearly that white servants were cruelly treated, ran away, were hunted down and branded, even as Negroes. The Servants' Plot came in 1663 but the big slave insurrection under Nat Turner did not come until 1831.[5] It is usually said that the Servants' Plot led to the effort to prohibit the importation of convicts; the Slave Rebellion to increased efforts to colonize emancipated slaves outside Virginia. During the early period of importation of Negroes into Virginia some of them gained their freedom by proving that they were in fact held by indenture. That there was logic in the contention is proved by the fact that in the early census lists Virginia Negroes were carried as servants and not as slaves. In the Virginia Code of 1860 there was a reference to "a Negro, who is a slave for a term of years." The old practice of apprenticing illegitimate children created a special class of Negro servants for a term of years who later became free. And there must have been large numbers of such Negro servants. . . .

Much of the early Virginia legislation, therefore, was concerned with both servants and slaves and the laws on runaways covered Negroes as well as whites. About the middle of the sixteen hundreds imported Negroes and the issue of Negro mothers became in law servants for life or slaves; but the number of free Negroes in the colony was increasing also. While there were some separate acts concerning slaves, servants, runaways, or free Negroes, many of the Virginia laws were enacted to cover all of these classes; some sections of a given law referred to all these groups, other sections to only one or perhaps two of the groups. Selections from the laws have been made as carefully as possible to preserve the original meaning and to cover the separate chapter headings of this volume. In the first and second volumes of Hening's

[5]See page 52 for mention of another Negro conspiracy.

compilation on early Virginia law, covering the years 1629-'82, slaves were not separately indexed, Negroes briefly, but servants at length. During the sixteen hundreds white servitude was of much greater importance in Virginia than slavery, and did not disappear until after the Revolution. Even in 1785 and 1792 there were acts concerning servants[6] and as late as 1824 there was an act on enticing servants and slaves away and on harboring servants and slaves. But that the Negro had practically displaced the white servant by the time of the Revolution is clear; the census of Virginia in 1782 listed 270,702 slaves and 296,852 free persons, of whom of course many were free Negro servants. In the present Virginia Code there are sections on apprenticeship which make interesting reading and which may be traced back law by law to the early indenture of homeless minors in Virginia. The forms of law change slowly, attitudes and practice much more readily.

As far as practical general laws have been split into the various separate subdivisions of this book but this was not always advisable. In fact none of the separate chapters of this summary should be regarded as complete in themselves nor mutually exclusive. Much of the material of this book because of the comprehensive character of the original enactments could be as reasonably included in any one of the several chapters as the one in which it is presented here. On the whole, however, it is thought that the attempt to arrange the material under the several rough categories has the advantage of increasing interest, readability, coherence, simplicity. It must be added that the old legislation is by no means always perfectly plain and a compendium of comment and criticism could profitably be worked out to accompany it. In an effort to retain as much of the old flavor as possible

---

[6]See pages 62, 65, 82 post.

liberties have not been taken with the original text unless it appeared unnecessarily long and repetitive. In a few instances, for the purpose of dramatic contrast or to complete the picture of a legal situation the same material is repeated in more than one chapter, but in general those who wish a complete statement on any subject should use the general index. No material has been digested in this book unless it has some definite bearing on the legal status of the Negro, but under the circumstances much of the material definitely affects white persons as well.

An effort has been made to assemble the law on free Negroes in Virginia but a word of explanation is necessary. Many of the laws were originally passed for the so-called better government of Negroes, bond as well as free. The free Negro before the Civil War lived in many respects under fixed legal disabilities the same as the slave. The important legal differences today in the position of the Virginia Negro and the Virginia white lie in the administration of the law and not the substantive law. The manumitted slave did not become a citizen and enjoyed few civil rights in Virginia. The Negro in the Old Dominion, whether indented servant, slave, free person of color or citizen, has always been an enormously disadvantaged human being. The writer who knows the law's inequalities administratively, the differences in school facilities for Negroes and whites, the heavy economic handicaps of Negroes, the inferior social work and welfare programs provided them is astonished that so many present-day Negroes are able to avoid the pitfalls in their white-made environment. Negroes do indeed furnish a disproportionate share of juvenile delinquents, criminals, illegitimates, venereally diseased, tuberculous, illiterates and unemployed, but that their showing is no worse is to their honor, when the details of their past and present are dispassionately considered.

The nature of human slavery led to many strange legal complications. In law a slave was a person who could commit a crime and be punished. He could under some circumstances be himself the subject of a homicide or a larceny. At the same time a slave was hardly a person at all but belonged legally in a classification of property. Virginia had much difficulty in deciding whether to place the slave in the category of real or personal property but the chattel nature of a slave became finally established. On account of being a piece of property a slave had no right legally to own property himself unless especially permitted to do so by his owner. As property the slave could not be a person and have a legal wife and children; as a natural person he was encouraged, not to say required, to have them illegitimately. As property a slave was assessed for taxation and as a quasi-person he was listed for tithes and poll taxes, the slave's owner of course actually being responsible for the payment of the taxes. Much of this legal confusion appears in the various chapters of this book and sheds not a little light on several current race problems.

In assembling this material the usual legal indices were used. But legal indices are notoriously inadequate and inconsistent and those in the books consulted were no exceptions. Page by page, therefore, Hening's statutes at large in thirteen volumes, Shepherd's in three volumes and the session laws published thereafter were carefully leafed through in an effort to pick up all the material bearing on slaves and Negroes. The Codes for 1819, 1873, 1860 and 1930 were used to discover possible omissions. The early habit of the Assembly in re-enacting an entire law when amending a portion of it makes it seem probable that little important material has been overlooked. Where year books for assemblies covered by Hening and Shepherd were found they were also made use of but of these not many were available. Shepherd's work was a continuation of Hening and his compilation ended with the acts passed in February, 1808. Shepherd used Arabic numerals.

For the most part, no mention is made in the book of sections repealing other sections; the successive laws show changes clearly enough for lay readers. It may be well to point out that this book is not intended for lawyers but primarily for those interested in the legal and historical sources of certain racial questions. Lawyers should use the unabridged acts in all cases. Occasionally the same or almost the same material is carried in this summary in several successive years to indicate the activity of the Assembly on various subjects or the little change which the years brought on some subjects. In a few cases notes call attention to matters not carried in the body of the book.

In a number of instances material was referred to in amendments which was not located in earlier session laws. On the other hand, material is included in this summary which was not always found in the Codes because of the repeal or amendment of acts before the re-printing of Codes. Court decisions interpreting or declaring laws unconstitutional are not cited. To have done so would have added much to the technical value of this volume. However, at the same time, this would have carried the work far into the legal field and so greatly increased its size that it could not have remained a simple, inexpensive handbook for the lay reader interested in present-day Negro problems. The book summarizes the actions of the Virginia Assembly only. Much racial psychology and history is thus given in a form which in no way reflects the personal opinions of the writer. Some may say that without a discussion of the social background in which laws are passed there can be little understanding of them. The writer feels that these laws, passed and re-passed by Virginians, as represented in their General Assembly, speak very eloquently for themselves. Anyway the writer is not an historian but a lawyer and social worker; besides there are many excellent histories of Virginia and slavery. In fact, there are hundreds of books about slavery and slaves and the legal and philosophic attitudes on the subject. There have been books which have attempted to summarize American slave law, as well. But such books are usually old, ponderous, incomplete, expensive, difficult to own.[7] None of them arranges material topically as well as chronologically nor brings subjects down to date. The Black Laws of Virginia merely claims to be a simple but rather comprehensive topical arrangement of Virginia law on Negroes compiled from the original legal sources. Those wishing to study the entire subject of slavery and Negro problems will necessarily refer as before to a great many other books.

The material is cited by the year of passage[8] rather than by the Assembly passing it. After the material was gathered the manuscript was put aside for a period of about two years and then rechecked to the original sources. Most of it was found with ease but in a few instances sections were located with difficulty because it should be noted different publications of the original laws used different systems of numbering; sometimes also there were extra sessions of the Assembly convening in the same year, making duplicate act-numbering for those years. Some of the old volumes contained no general index but did have several poorly arranged indices dotted through thick volumes Paging in some books

[7] An excellent recent book is the three volume summary of *case decisions* of English and American courts, "Judicial Cases Concerning American Slavery and the Negro," by Catterall, which brings Virginia decisions down to 1875.
[8] This was done as a simple way of indicating year to year changes in the law. Occasionally this method may add to the difficulty of finding the original acts cited. For instance, the Assembly convening December 6, 1819, in January, 1820, passed Chapter CXVI, and the Assembly convening December 4, 1820, on December 21, 1820, passed Chapter 116; cited on page 81.

was irregular; sometimes the numbering of acts was not consistent; often the numbers of acts passed late in a year were smaller than the number of acts passed earlier in the same year. Readers attempting to locate original passages need not be discouraged, all the material included here will be found in the original books but occasionally a searcher may need to go armed with a search warrant. To give an example of some of the difficulties encountered by one who delves in old Virginia law books: In Volume 1808-15 of the Acts of the Assembly, Act LXXXIV, passed in February, 1814, will be found printed on page one hundred and forty-one in about the middle of the volume, but on page one hundred and forty, about one hundred and forty pages farther on will be found another chapter, LXXXIV, passed in November, 1814. Nor do the years always come consecutively in the original laws. To give one other random example, an act of February, 1821, is to be found on page one hundred and twenty-four, and an act of February, 1820, on page one hundred and thirty-four of the Acts of 1819-23.

Some sessions of the Assembly used Arabic and some Roman numbering; occasionally in the same year both would be used; different compilers or printers used different systems. In this book the numbering has been retained as it appears in the books consulted. Old capitalization and spelling have been for the most part discarded. As far as possible the laws have been either digested and restated in a simple modern form or pertinent material has been abstracted or lifted bodily from the original. In some cases the English used by the Assembly was so confused that no change has been made for fear of changing the original sense, whatever it may have been. Something of the old flavor has perhaps been retained by the use of the same construction and terminology wherever this seemed practical.

Prior to about 1680 the word Negro was used in the original Virginia laws but thereafter the word mulatto was also used. In this summary Negro is usually made to cover Negro and mulatto. Mulatto was first separately indexed in Hening's third volume covering the years 1682-1710 and the indexing there covered over one-half column. In the second volume of Hening, the reader was referred from mulatto to Negro. Actually mulattoes were found in Virginia much earlier than this as a reference to Chapter I of this compilation makes very clear. Mulatto is of later use in the law and tended to disappear as a distinctive legal concept, with the increase in the actual number of such people in the state. In Virginia, at the present time, the number of full-blooded Negroes uncontaminated by a drop of white blood is probably not very great.

In the Virginia Code of 1860 Negroes were indexed to the extent of almost a page, slaves almost two pages, runaways one-half page, and mulattoes as: see definitions of mulatto and Negro, see slaves, see free Negroes; mulatto then meant legally the same as Negro. At the outbreak of the Civil War the population of Virginia was 1,596,318, of which 548,907 or over one-third were Negroes. Of the Negroes 58,042 were free and 490,865 were slaves. By the last census Virginia had a population of 2,421,851, of whom 650,165 were Negroes.

It is the custom in Virginia, as everywhere in the South, to blame the Negro for the extent of social problems; high crime rates, high illegitimacy rates, high illiterary rates, high tuberculosis rates, high venereal disease rates, high unemployment and relief rates; all the prevalent serious social inadequacies of the South are cooly laid at the door of the Negro. But much of the Negro's heredity and all of his social environment are the result of white aggression and white discrimination. In spite of ancient but ever more drastic penalties for interbreeding, miscegenation continues in Virginia. In spite of early efforts to prohibit the importation of slaves and discourage the residence of free Negroes the Black Virginian, like a Black Albatross, is hung around the neck of the Old Dominion. What holy man shall shrieve her soul?

JUNE PURCELL GUILD.

Richmond, Virginia
December 1, 1936.

CHAPTER I

The Struggle for Racial Integrity

1607-1630. James Citty or Cittie, later called Jamestown, was settled in 1607.[1] The first Virginia Assembly convened there in June, 1619. Negroes were landed from a Dutch trading ship for the first time in the same year.[2] Few records remain of the laws or orders passed prior to the year 1629 and Hening's compilation of Virginia law begins with 1629. The first reference to a Negro in this early legislation is found under date of September 17, 1630. And in this first enactment concerning a Negro, Virginia began her long fight against the interbreeding and intermarriage of Negroes and whites. Hening's extract from the minutes of the judicial proceedings of the governor and the council of Virginia reads: Hugh Davis to be soundly whipped, before an assembly of Negroes and others for abusing himself to the dishonor of God and shame of Christians by defiling his body in lying with a Negro, which fault he is to acknowledge next Sabbath day.

1640. From the minutes of the proceedings of the governor and council of Virginia, reprinted by Hening from a manuscript originally belonging to Jefferson: Robert Sweet to do penance in church according to the laws of England, for getting a Negro woman with a child and the woman whipt.

[1] Not even the original name of the first English settlement in Virginia survives.

[2] The date is sometimes cited 1620. It should be remembered that early dates are often quoted in different years because of the change in the English calendar in the fifteen hundreds. For other important importations of this period see the Introduction.

1642. Chapter XX. Whereas many great abuses have been found to arise both against the law of God and likewise to the servants of many masters through the secret marriages[3] of servants as also by committing fornification, it is enacted, the consent of the master must be obtained for marriage under penalty of extension of time; fornication also is likewise punishable, freemen to pay tobacco.

1645. Act II. Adultery, whoredom, fornification, and drunkness shall be reported by church wardens, for neglect they shall be fined by county courts; and courts neglecting shall be fined by the governor and council.[4]

1657. Act II. A person guilty of drunkenness, blasphemous cursing, swearing, adultery, fornification, is made incapable of being a witness or holding any public office; penalty for first offense of drunkenness, fifty pounds of tobacco, swearing twelve pounds of tobacco; servants and minors are to be referred to the county courts for correction if parents or masters refuse to pay the fine.

1657. Act XIV. Servants marrying without the consent of their masters are to serve one year after their term has expired; a free man marrying a servant woman is to pay double the value of the extra service, a man servant committing fornification with a woman servant is to serve her master one year or pay 1,500 pounds of tobacco and give security to indemnify the parish against the expense of the child. A freeman so offending shall pay 1,500 pounds of tobacco or one year's service to the master of the servant of whom he

---

[3]As early as 1631, by Act VI it was provided that no minister celebrate matrimony between any persons without a license except the banns have been first published three several Sundays, nor join any persons except between 8 and 12 in the forenoon, and no license necessary if the parties are under 21 years and the parents personally consent.
[4]Similar act passed in 1642.

shall get a bastard child and give security to maintain the child. Fornication is punished by paying 500 pounds of tobacco to the use of the parish or by whipping.

1660. Act XXIX; 1661. Acts XII; XCIX. The laws are amended on the secret marriages of servants, servants running away, hiring servants without certificates, etc.

1662. Act VI. Whereas, by act of the Assembly a woman servant having a bastard is to serve two extra years and late experience shows that some dissolute masters have gotten their maids with child and claim the benefit of their service, and on the contrary if the woman got with child by the master be freed of service, it might induce such loose persons to lay all their bastards to their masters, it is enacted that each woman servant got with child by her master shall after her indenture is expired be sold for two years by the church wardens, the tobacco to be employed by the vestry for the use of the parish.

1662. Act VIII. Whereas, the punishment of a reputed father of a bastard child is keeping the child and saving the parish harmless, if it should happen the reputed father be a servant who can no way accomplish the penalty, it is enacted, that men servants getting a child the parish shall take care of the child during the father's service, and that after he is free the reputed father shall make satisfaction to the parish.

1662. Act XII. Children got by an Englishman upon a Negro woman shall be bond or free according to the condition of the mother, and if any Christian shall commit fornication with a Negro man or woman, he shall pay double the fines of a former act.[5]

1691. Act XI. The preamble recites that the many good laws made before for prohibiting swearing, Sabbath abusing, drunkenness, fornication and adultery have not produced the desired effect; fines and stocks are ordered for offenders.

1691. Act XVI. This act provides penalties because many times Negroes, mulattoes and other slaves unlawfully absent themselves from their masters' and mistresses' service and lie hid and lurk in obscure places, killing hogs and committing other injuries.

And for prevention of that abominable mixture and spurious issue which hereafter may increase as well by Negroes, mulattoes and Indians intermarrying with English, or other white women, it is enacted that for the time to come, that whatsoever English or other white man or woman, bond or free, shall intermarry with a Negro, mulatto, or Indian man or woman, bond or free, he shall within three months be banished from this dominion forever.

And it is further enacted, that if any English woman being free shall have a bastard child by a Negro she shall pay fifteen pounds to the church wardens, and in default of such payment, she shall be taken into possession by the church wardens and disposed of for five years and the amount she brings shall be paid one-third to their majesties for the support of the government, one-third to the of the parish where the offense is committed and the other third to the informer. The child shall be bound out by the church wardens until he is

_____
[5]Prior to this date the legal position of the Negro in Virginia was vague but was regulated generally by laws controlling indentured servants.

thirty years of age. In case the English woman that shall
have a bastard is a servant, she shall be sold by the church
wardens (after her time is expired) for five years, and the
child serve as aforesaid.

1696. Act. I. This act mentions the same difficulties and
names special penalties for the fornification and adultery of
servants and repeats the historic passage, Be it enacted that
all children born in the country be bond or free according to
the condition of the mother.

1705. Act XLIX. This act, on servants and slaves, states that
for a further Christian care of all Christian slaves it is enacted that no Negro, mulatto or Indian, although Christian,
or Jew, Moor, Mohammedan or other infidel, shall purchase
any Christian servant nor any other except of their own complexion, or such as are declared slaves, but if any Negro or
other infidel or such as are declared slaves (i. e., those not
Christians in their native country, except Turks and Moors in
amity) shall notwithstanding purchase any Christian white
servant the said servant shall become free, ipso facto, and if any
person having such Christian white servant shall intermarry
with any such Negro, mulatto or Indian, Jew, Moor, Mohammedan or other infidel, every Christian white servant of
every such person so intermarrying shall, ipso facto, become
free and acquit from any service due to such master or mistress so intermarrying. A woman servant having a bastard
shall for every offense serve her owner one whole year after
her indenture has expired or pay 1,000 pounds of tobacco,
and the reputed father, if free, shall give security to the
church wardens to maintain the child, but if a servant, he
shall make satisfaction to the parish after his indenture has

expired. And if any woman servant shall be got with baby by her master, she shall be sold by the church wardens for one year after her indenture, or pay 1,000 pounds in tobacco. If a woman servant has a bastard by a Negro, or mulatto she shall pay for the use of the parish 15 pounds current money or be sold for five years at the expiration of her time. If a free Christian white woman should have a bastard child, she shall pay 15 pounds current money of Virginia or be sold for five years. In both cases the church wardens shall bind the child to be a servant until it shall be thirty-one years of age.

Whatsoever white man or woman being free shall intermarry with a Negro shall be committed to prison for six months without bail, and pay 10 pounds to the use of the parish. Ministers marrying such persons shall pay 10,000 pounds of tobacco.

1710. Chapter XII. If any white or other woman not being a slave be delivered of a bastard child and she endeavor to avoid shame and punishment by drowning or secret burying to conceal the death, the mother so offending shall suffer death, except such mother can make proof that the child was born dead; this act is to be read yearly in churches by the ministers under penalty of 500 pounds of tobacco for omission.[*]

1753. Chapter VII. A woman servant having a bastard child shall serve one extra year or pay her master 1,000 pounds of tobacco and the reputed father, if free, shall give security to the church wardens for the child's maintenance and keep the parish indemnified; if a servant he shall make satisfaction after his time of indenture. If a woman servant be got with a child by her master when her time is expired, she shall be

---
[*]Repealed in 1819.

sold by the church wardens for one year. If any woman servant has a bastard child by a Negro over the year due her master, she shall upon the expiration of her time be sold for five years or pay 15 pounds current money. If a free Christian white woman shall have a bastard child by a Negro, or mulatto, for every such offense she shall pay to the church wardens 15 pounds current money or be by them sold for five years and the church wardens shall bind the child to be a servant until it shall be thirty-one years of age. Whatsoever English, or white man or woman being free shall intermarry with a Negro or mulatto man or woman, bond or free, shall be committed to prison for six months without bail and pay 10 pounds to the use of the parish.

1765. Chapter XXIV. Bastard children of woman servants and Negroes or free Christian, white women by Negroes, shall hereafter be bound out, the males to serve until twenty-one years of age and the females to serve until eighteen years of age, only and no longer; the former law binding the child out until thirty-one years of age now declared an unreasonable severity to such children.

1769. Chapter XXVII. Whereas the laws now in force are not sufficient for the security and indemnification of the parishes from the great charges frequently arising from children begotten and born out of lawful matrimony: For remedy, it is enacted that if any single woman, not being a servant or slave, shall be delivered of a bastard child likely to be chargeable to any parish, and shall charge any person, not a servant, with being the father of the child, a warrant shall be issued, and the person so charged shall be committed to jail unless he enters into a recognizance with security to appear

and perform the orders of the court. If the person is adjudged the father of a bastard child, he may be charged with
the payment of money or tobacco for its maintenance, in such
manner and for such time as the child is likely to become
chargeable to the parish. A recognizance with sureties for
the maintenance of the child shall be given. If the father
refuses to enter into the recognizance, he shall be committed
to the common jail, there to remain without bail until he shall
enter the recognizance or shall discharge himself by taking
the oath of an insolvent debtor.

It is further enacted that if any single woman not being a
servant shall be delivered of a bastard child she shall be liable
to pay the sum of twenty shillings to the church wardens,
but the persons so convicted shall not be liable to be whipped
for failing to pay.

Bastard children shall be bound out by the church wardens
if male to the age of twenty-one, if female to eighteen years.

Whereas it frequently happens that convict servants are
delivered of bastards, who being disabled to give testimony
cannot be examined, nor for that reason can the reputed
father of a bastard child be discovered and the parish indemnified from the charge of its maintenance: for remedy it is
enacted that where any convict servant woman shall be delivered of a bastard child, during the time of her service, the
master or owner of such servant shall be obliged to maintain
such child and in consideration of such maintenance shall be
entitled to the service of the child to twenty-one years if male,
and eighteen if female.

1785. Chapter IV. It is provided that counties shall have
district overseers of the poor. The powers of church wardens

in relation to the poor and bastards are transferred to the overseers.

1785. Chapter LX. An act directing the course of descents declares that bastards shall inherit or transmit inheritance on part of the mother, and when a man has a child by a woman and afterwards intermarries with her, the child, if recognized by him, shall be legitimate. The issue also of marriages deemed null in law shall nevertheless be legitimate.

1785. Chapter LXXVIII. Every person of whose grandfathers or grandmothers anyone is or shall have been a Negro, although all his other progenitors, except that descending from the Negro shall have been white persons, shall be deemed a mulatto, and so every person who shall have one-fourth or more Negro blood shall in like manner be deemed a mulatto. This act is to be in force from January 1, 1787.

1792. Chapter 40. This act providing for the poor, and declaring who shall be vagrants, states that the overseers shall provide for the poor, lame, blind and other inhabitants of the district not able to maintain themselves and may also provide poor houses, nurses and doctors.

The court is authorized to direct the overseers to bind out poor orphans and children apprenticed to such persons as the court shall approve until twenty-one years old, if a boy, or eighteen years, if a girl.

If any single woman, not being a servant or slave, shall be delivered of a bastard child which shall be chargeable or likely to become chargeable to any county, and shall upon oath charge any person, not being a servant, with being the father, it shall be lawful, upon application of the overseers, for a warrant to be issued for the person so charged, and he may be committed to jail, unless he enters into a recognizance, in the sum of $30.00 to appear, at next term of court. If the child is likely to become chargeable to the county, the father may be ordered to pay for the child's maintenance.

Every bastard child may be apprenticed to twenty-one years, if a male, or eighteen years, if a female.

1792. Chapter 41. It is provided that every person other than a Negro, although all his other progenitors, except that descending from the Negro shall have been white persons shall be deemed a mulatto; so every such person who shall have one-fourth part or more of Negro blood, shall in like manner be deemed a mulatto.[7]

1792. Chapter 42. For preventing white men and white women intermarrying with Negroes or mulattoes, it is enacted that whatsoever white man or woman, being free, shall intermarry with a Negro man or woman, bond or free, he or she shall be committed to prison for six months, and pay $30.00 for the use of the parish.

The penalty for a minister marrying Negroes and whites is set at $250.00 for every such marriage.

Whatsoever person shall take a woman against her will shall be guilty of a felony, provided that this act shall not extend to any person taking any woman, only claiming her as his ward or bond-woman.

1792. Chapter 72. Every person not being a servant or slave committing adultery or fornication, and being convicted by

---

[7]The Code of 1860, Chap. 103, reads: Every person who has one-fourth or more of Negro blood shall be deemed a mulatto, and the word Negro in any section shall be construed to mean mulatto as well as Negro.

the oaths of two or more credible witnesses or confession of the party, shall forfeit $20.00 for adultery and $10.00 for fornication.

1803. Chapter 6. The marriage between Benjamin Butt, Jr., and a certain Lydia Bright, who is of respectable family, and was at the time of the marriage supposed to be unsullied in her reputation, is dissolved because Lydia has been delivered of a mulatto child and has publicly acknowledged that the father of the child is a slave.

1804. Chapter 15. The recognizance for his appearance of a person charged with being the father of a bastard shall be in a sum of not less than $50.00 nor more than $200.00. If the bond is forfeited, it shall be paid to the overseers for the use of the poor.

1805. Chapter 11. The proceeding in bastardy continues to be entitled an act providing for the poor and declaring who shall be vagrants, and is limited by its terms to single white women, who charge any person not being a servant with being the father of a bastard child. The father may be ordered to maintain the child as long as it is likely to become chargeable to the town.[8]

1814. Chapter XCVIII. A marriage solemnized between Richard Jones, of the County of Northampton, and his wife, Peggy, is dissolved and Richard forever divorced from Peggy provided that a jury find that the child of Peggy is not the child of Richard, but is the offspring of a man of color.

---

[8]In the Codes of 1819, 1860, and 1873, this law is limited to "any unmarried white women" but a note in 1873 states that the word "free" has been stricken out as inconsistent with the Constitution of the state and the United States.

1818. Chapter XVIII. One leaving the state to avoid certain sections of the marriage law of 1792 shall be guilty as if the offense were committed in this Commonwealth.

1833. Chapter 80. A court upon satisfactory proof, by a white person of the fact, may grant to any free person of mixed blood a certificate that he is not a Negro, which certificate shall protect such person against the penalties and disabilities to which free Negroes are subject.

1833. Chapter 243. Certain parties named Wharton, of the County Stafford, who heretofore were held in slavery and acquired their freedom since 1806 are not Negroes or mulattoes but white persons, although remotely descended from a colored woman, and are hereby released from all penalties whatsoever, by reason of their failure to remove from the Commonwealth.

1848. Criminal Code. Chapter 120. Any free person who shall commit adultery shall be fined. Any white person having a former spouse who shall marry another shall'be punished. Any white persons who shall intermarry with a Negro shall be confined in jail not more than twelve months and fined not exceeding $100.00. The person performing the ceremony shall be fined not less than $200.00.

1853. Chapter 25. Every commissioner of the revenue shall make an annual registration of the births and deaths in his district. He shall record the date and place of every birth, the full name of the child, the sex and color, and if colored whether free or slave, the full name of the mother, and if the child be free and born in wedlock the full name, occupation and residence of the father, if the child be a slave, the name of the owner, etc.

1866. Chapter 17. Every person having one-fourth or more Negro blood shall be deemed a colored person, and every person not a colored person having one-fourth or more Indian blood shall be deemed an Indian.

1866. Chapter 18. It shall be the duty of every minister celebrating a marriage and of the keeper of the records of any religious society which solemnizes marriages, by the consent of the parties in open congregation at once to make a record of every marriage between white persons, or between colored persons, stating in such record whether the persons are white or colored, and to return a copy to the clerk of the county or corporation in which the marriage is solemnized.

Where colored persons have agreed to occupy the relation of husband and wife and shall be cohabiting together as such at the time of this act, whether the rites of marriage have been celebrated between them or not, they shall be deemed husband and wife and their children legitimate. When the parties have ceased to cohabit before the passage of this act in consequence of the death of the woman or from any other cause, all the children of the woman, recognized by the man to be his, shall be deemed legitimate.

1867. Chapter 127. It having been represented to the Assembly that the United States authorities have collected statistics exhibiting the marriages heretofore solemnized between colored persons which ought to be preserved, and the Assembly being solicitous to preserve evidences for legitimizing the offspring of such marriages, the governor is instructed to obtain from the United States authorities registers of marriages between colored persons and have copies deposited with clerks of courts.[9]

1867-1870. Constitution of Virginia. Article XI, Section 9. The children of slave parents, who were recognized by the father as his children, and whose mother was recognized by such father as his wife, shall be capable of inheriting any estates whereof the father may have died siezed, as though they had been born in lawful wedlock.

1873. Chapter 148. If the court shall adjudge the accused to be the father of a bastard child, it shall order him to pay to the overseers of the poor for the maintenance of said child, such sums as it may deem proper for each year until such time as the court may appoint. The court shall order the father to give bond.

1875. Chapter 112. The Code of 1873 in relation to the maintenance of illegitimate children is hereby repealed.[10]

1878. Chapter 311. Under the subject of offences against morality and decency, it is said: If any white or Negro resident of the state shall go out of the state for the purpose of being married, and with the intention of returning, be married out of it, and return, he shall be as guilty as if the marriage had been in the state.

Any white person who shall intermarry with a Negro, or any Negro who shall intermarry with a white person, shall be confined in the penitentiary from two to five years.

---

[9]Passed in April.
[10]There is no support law in Virginia at the present time for illegitimate children.

1879. Chapter 252. All marriages between a white person and a Negro shall be absolutely void without any decree of divorce or other legal process.[11]

1910. Chapter 357. Every person having one-sixteenth or more Negro blood shall be deemed a colored person, and every person not a colored person having one-fourth or more of Indian blood shall be deemed an Indian.[12]

1924. Chapter 371. For the preservation of racial integrity, registration certificates shall be made out and filed for those persons born before June 14, 1912, showing the racial mixture for whom a birth certificate is not on file. It is a penitentiary offence to make a registration certificate false as to race or color. No marriage license shall be granted unless the clerk has reasonable assurance that the statements as to color are correct.

It shall be unlawful for any white person to marry any save a white person, or a person with no other admixture of blood than white and American Indian. The term "white person" shall apply only to the person who has no trace whatsoever of any blood other than Caucasian, but persons who have one-sixteenth or less of the blood of the American Indian, and no other non-Caucasic blood shall be deemed white persons. All laws heretofore passed and in effect regarding the intermarriage of white and colored persons shall apply to marriages prohibited by this act.

1930. Chapter 85. Every person in whom there is ascertainable any Negro blood shall be deemed a colored person, and every person not a colored person having one-fourth or more

[11]The same is found in the Code of 1860; in the Code of 1873, and in the present Code.
[12]Amends paragraph 49 of Virginia Code.

American Indian blood shall be deemed an American Indian; except that members of Indian tribes living on reservations allotted them by Virginia, having one-fourth or more of Indian blood and less than one-sixteenth of Negro blood, shall be deemed tribal Indians so long as they are domiciled on reservations.

1932. Chapter 78. If any white person intermarry with a colored person, or any colored person intermarry with a white person, he shall be guilty of a felony and confined in the penitentiary for from one to five years.

CHAPTER II

Servants and Slaves in the Sixteen Hundreds

1623.   No person upon rumor of supposed change shall presume to be disobedient to the present government, nor servants to their private officers, masters or overseers at their uttermost peril.

Every freeman shall fence a quarter of an acre of land to make a garden for planting vines and herbs and mulberry trees.

1639. Act X. All persons except Negroes[1] are to be provided with arms and ammunition or be fined at the pleasure of the governor and council.

1642. Act XXI. This section recites that complaints have been made against divers persons who entertain and enter into covenants with runaway servants and freemen who formerly hired themselves to others, to the prejudice if not the utter undoing of divers poor men, also thereby encouraging servants to run from their masters. It provides a penalty to the person hiring them of twenty pounds of tobacco if the hiring is made without certificate.

1642. Act XXII. A punishment is provided for loitering runaways in the colony; for a second offense a runaway is to be branded in the cheek with the letter "R."

It is a felony for a runaway to carry powder and shot, punishable by death.

---

[1] This appears to be the second direct reference to a Negro in Virginia legislation. For the first mention see Chapter I, page 1.

If there is a complaint of the master for harsh or un-Christian usage or for want of diet, the commissioner may warn the master or mistress.

1642. Act XXVI. Servants brought in without indentures shall, if above twenty years serve four years, if they be above twelve years and under twenty years, five years, and if under twelve, seven years.

1642. Act XLI. Masters of every family shall bring to church on Sundays one serviceable gun under penalty of ten pounds of tobacco, and a servant commanded and yet omitting shall receive twenty lashes on his bare shoulders.

1642. Act LX. Whereas at an Assembly in October, 1639,[2] in consideration that divers ill-disposed persons, did covertly trade and truck with other men's servants and apprentices, which tended to the injury of masters of families, their servants being thereby induced to purloin the goods of their masters, it is enacted that what persons should buy or trade, with any servant for any commodity without consent of the master of the servant, they should be imprisoned for one month and forfeit to the master of the servant four times the value of the thing bought.

1654. Act VI. Irish servants brought in without indentures, if above sixteen years old, are to serve six years; if under sixteen years, to serve until twenty-four years of age.[3]

1655. Act I. Indian children brought in as hostages are not to be treated as slaves.[4]

---

[2]Not found in Hening.

[3]By Act LXXXV, 1657, there is added at the end of the above act, "and all aliens to be included in this act." Because the act discouraged many from coming to Virginia on account of the length of time to serve, the act was repealed in 1659. "In future no servant coming from a Christian country shall serve longer than those of our own country."

[4]This appears to be the first use of the word *slave* in Virginia legislation.

1657. Act XVIII.   Whereas divers controversies have arisen, it is enacted that servants without indenture, if over sixteen years, shall serve four years; if under fifteen years, until twenty-one years of age.

1657. Act XLVIII. Indian children confided to any person for education or instruction in the Christian religion or for learning English shall not be assigned or transferred, and such Indian children shall be free at the age of twenty-five years.

1657. Act CXI.   It is enacted that no person shall dare to buy any Indian from the English and in case of complaint shall return such Indian within ten days to the place from whence he was taken.

1657. Act CXIII.   Whereas hue and cry after runaway servants has been much neglected to the great loss of the inhabitants, it is enacted that all such hue and cry shall be signed either by the governor or some of the council and the same shall be conveyed from house to house with all convenient speed. Runaways, if found, shall be sent from constable to constable until delivered to their master or mistress.

1658. Act III. It is provided that the master of every runaway shall cut the hair of all such runaways close above the ears, whereby they may be with more ease discovered and apprehended.

1659. Act XIII.   It is enacted that when a servant shall lay violent hands on his master and is convicted thereof, the court is authorized to order such servant to serve his master two years after his time by indenture, custom, or law has expired.

1660. Act XXII. It is enacted that in case any English servant shall run away in company with any Negroes who are incapable of making satisfaction by addition of time,[5] that the English so running away shall serve for the time of the Negroes' absence as they are to do for their own by a former act.

1661. Act XV. Whereas the private burial of servants and others gives occasion of much scandal against divers persons and sometimes not undeservedly of being guilty of their deaths, be it enacted that there be in every parish three or more places set apart for places of public burial, and before the corpse be buried there, three or four neighbors be called who may view the corpse, and no person, whether free or servant, shall be buried in any other place except by his own appointment.

1661. Act XCII. Whereas the excessive prices exacted by "diverse avaritious and gripeing practitioners in phisick and chirurgery" has caused several hard-hearted masters to expose sick servants to a hazard of recovery than put themselves to the certain charge of a rigorous though unskilful physician, whose demands for the most part exceed the purchase of the patient, many other poor people being forced to give themselves to a lingering disease, it is enacted that it shall be lawful for any person conceiving the account of a physician or surgeon unreasonable to arrest the said physician or surgeon to the general court, and the court may allow a 50

---

[5]This must mean *slaves* and is one of the earliest legal references to servitude for life in Virginia. Actually some Negroes were being sold for life in Virginia twenty years before this time. For the first direct reference to *Negro slaves* in the law of Virginia see 1659, Act XVI, post, Chapter VI.

per cent advance over the true value of the drugs administered.[6]

1661. CIII. Whereas the barbarous usage of some servants by cruel masters brings so much scandal and infamy to the country that people who would adventure hither are through fear diverted, it is enacted that every master shall provide servants with competent diet, clothing, lodging, and shall not exceed the bounds of moderation in correcting them and a servant may make complaint to the commissioner and have remedy for his grievances.[7]

1661. Act CIV. Unruly and incorrigible servants who resist their masters and overseers and lay hands on them shall be required by the court to serve their masters one year after their term is expired.

1661. Act CXXXVIII. It is enacted that what Englishman, trader, or other shall bring in any Indians as servants and shall assign them over to any other, they shall not sell them for slaves nor for any longer time than English of like ages should serve and no person shall entertain any neighboring Indians as servants unless by a license from the governor.

1662.[8] Act II. Whereas many servants bring in goods or have them sent to them, which usually the party which imports them or those to whom they are sold as servants, convert to their own use, it is enacted that servants shall have the property in their own goods.

---

[6] The law permitting the arrest of physicians was repealed in 1692, and physicians were thereafter allowed 100 percent above the true value of the drugs furnished.
[7] Such laws as these indicate that the position of the indentured servant was no better than that of a slave at this time.
[8] For the passage in 1662 establishing the rule that children are bond or free according to the condition of their mother, see Chapter I.

1663. An Assembly resolution of September 16 grants Birkenhead his freedom and 5,000 pounds of tobacco for having
discovered a horrid plot, and his master is to be satisfied for
his time.

In the same year the Assembly resolves that September 13
be annually kept holy, being the day those villains intended to
put the plot in execution.[9]

1663. Act VIII. Runaway servants are to be pursued at public expense, and letters written to the Dutch (Northern)
plantations to make seizure of fugitive servants.

1663. Act XVIII. For the better suppressing of unlawful
meetings of servants it is injoined that all masters take special
care that their servants do not depart from their houses on
Sundays or any other days without particular license.

1666. Act IX. The penalty is increased for harboring runaway servants who serve by their first indenture.

1667. Act III. Whereas some doubts have arisen whether
children that are slaves by birth, and by the charity and pity of
their owners made partakers of the blessed sacrament of
baptism, should by virtue of their baptism be made free, it is
enacted that baptism does not alter the condition of the person as to his bondage or freedom; masters freed from this
doubt may more carefully propagate Christianity by permitting slaves to be admitted to that sacrament.

1668. Act IV. The infliction of moderate corporal punishment on a runaway servant does not deprive the master of

[9]Negroes were not involved in the plot. Birkenhead was a white indentured servant,
probably a convict. See note to 1670, post, page 43.

extension of service, the one being as necessary to reclaim the servant as the other.

1669. Act I.   If a slave resist his master and by the extremity of the correction, chance to die, his death shall not be a felony, since it cannot be presumed that malice (which alone makes murder a felony) would induce a man to destroy his own estate.

1669. Act VIII.   A reward of 1,000 pounds of tobacco for anyone who apprehends a runaway servant is established. After the servant's time of service is up he shall be sold to reimburse the public for the tobacco paid the taker-up.

1670. April 20.   Extract from Legislative, Executive, and Judicial Proceedings of Governor and Council of Virginia, as contained in records of the General Court: The complaints of several of the council and others representing their apprehensions and fears, least the honor of his majesty and the peace of his colony be too much hazarded and endangered by the great number of felons and other desperate villains sent here from the several prisons in England, being this day read in Council, we have upon most serious and careful consideration thought fit to order and do accordingly order that for preventing and avoiding the danger which apparently threatens us from the barbarous designs and felonious practices of such wicked villains, that it shall not be permitted to bring in and land any jail-birds or such others who for notorious offenses shall deserve to die in England.[10]

---

[10]Hening says that because of the plot of convicts to gain their freedom from servitude in 1663, that the further importation of that class of people was prohibited. After this act the number of Negroes imported began to increase and during the 18th century the slave trade became very lively. However, convicts continued to come. See Chapter VII, 1788, page 63, post.

1670. Act I. This law concerning runaways recites that a former act for apprehending runaways has seemed too burdensome, and it is therefore enacted that the sum of 1,000 pounds of tobacco for a reward for taking up a runaway is reduced to 200 pounds and that the servant not being a slave (slaves are also comprehended in this act) after the expiration of his time shall serve four months for every 200 pounds of tobacco paid for apprehending; that a servant who has run away twice shall have his hair cut close under a penalty for the master for neglecting this; that every constable into whose hands a fugitive passes, shall whip him severely.

1670. Act V. Negroes or Indians, though baptised and enjoying their own freedom, shall be incapable of purchasing Christians, yet they are not debarred from buying any of their own color.

1670. Act XII. Whereas some dispute has arisen whether Indians taken in war by any other nation and by the nation that taketh them sold to the English are servants for life or a term of years, it is enacted that all servants not being Christians imported by shipping shall be slaves for their lives, but what shall come by land shall serve, if boys or girls, until thirty years of age; if men or women, twelve years and no longer.

1671. Act IV. In a former act it is provided that sheep, horses, cattle should be delivered in kind to an orphan when he comes of age, to which some have desired that Negroes be added; this Assembly considering the difficulty of procuring Negroes in kind as also the value and hazard of their lives has doubted whether any sufficient men could be found who would engage themselves to deliver Negroes of equal ages if the special Negroes should die, or become by age or accident unserviceable; it is enacted, that at discretion of the courts, Negroes may be appraised, sold at an outcry, or preserved in kind, as it is deemed most expedient for the preservation or advancement of the estates of orphans.

1676. Act I.[11]   All Indians taken in war shall be held and accounted slaves during life, and if any differences shall arise in cases about plunder or slaves, the chief commander of the party taking such slaves or plunder is to be the sole judge thereof to make equal division as he shall see fit.

1676. Act XII.   This act concerns servants who were out in rebellion with Nathaniel Bacon or Joseph Ingram and makes them punishable as runaways.[12]

1676.   An order at the General Assembly begun at Greene Spring, the 20th of February: All soldiers who take prisoners of Indian enemies may retain and keep all such Indian slaves.

1679. Act I.   Indian prisoners or plunder taken in war shall be free purchase to the soldier taking them.

1680. Act V.   For the encouragement of trade and manufacture, it is provided that all goods, wares, English servants, Negroes and other slaves imported after September 29, 1681, shall be landed and laid on shore, bought and sold at appointed places, and at no other places under penalty.

1680. Act X.   Whereas the frequent meetings of considerable numbers of Negro slaves under pretense of feasts and burials is judged of dangerous consequence, it is enacted that

[11] A Bacon's Rebellion enactment.
[12] Repealed in 1680.

no Negro or slave may carry arms, such as any club, staff, gun, sword, or other weapon, nor go from his owner's plantation without a certificate and then only on necessary occasions; the punishment twenty lashes on the bare back, well laid on. And, further, if any Negro lift up his hand against any Christian he shall receive thirty lashes, and if he absent himself or lie out from his master's service and resist lawful apprehension, he may be killed and this law shall be published every six months.

1682. Act I. It is enacted that all servants, except Turks and Moors, while in amity with his majesty which shall be imported into this country either by sea or by land, whether Negroes, Moors, mulattoes or Indians who and whose parentage and native countries are not Christian at the time of their first purchase by some Christian, although afterward and before their importation into this country they shall be converted to the Christian faith; and all Indians, which shall be sold by our neighboring Indians, or any others trafficing with us for slaves, are hereby adjudged deemed and taken to be slaves to all intents and purposes any law, usage, or custom to the contrary notwithstanding.

1682. Act III. Whereas the act of 1680 on Negro insurrection has not had the intended effect, it is enacted that church wardens read this and the other act, twice every year, in the time of divine service, or forfeit each of them six hundred pounds of tobacco, and further to prevent insurrections no master or overseer shall allow a Negro slave of another to remain on his plantation above four hours without leave of the slave's own master.

1691. Act IX. It is enacted that there be a free and open trade with all Indians and at all times.[13]

1691. Act XVI. An act for suppressing outlying slaves covering divers subjects, states whereas many times Negroes, mulattoes and other slaves lie hid and lurk in obscure places killing hogs and committing other injuries, it is enacted, that the sheriff may raise so many forces from time to time as he shall think convenient for the effectual apprehending of such Negroes. If they resist or runaway they may be killed or destroyed by gun or otherwise whatsoever, provided that the owner of any slave killed shall be paid four thousand pounds of tobacco by the public.

A great inconvenience may happen to this country by the setting of Negroes and mulattoes free, by their entertaining Negroes from their masters' service, or receiving stolen goods, or being grown old bringing a charge upon the country, it is enacted that no Negroes, or mulattoes be set free by any person whatsoever, unless such person pay for the transportation of such Negro out of the country within six months after such setting free, upon penalty of ten pounds sterling to the church wardens, with which the church wardens are to cause the Negro to be transported out of the country and the remainder given to the use of the poor of the parish.

---

[13]For years this law was lost sight of due to the fact that there was no edition of the laws printed in Virginia until 1733. It was afterward held to have abolished Indian slavery; in the meantime descendants of Indians had been enslaved.

CHAPTER III

Slaves and Servants in the Seventeen Hundreds

1701. Act II.   Whereas a Negro man named Billy, one time slave to John Tillet, Thomas Middleton, James Bray, gentlemen, has unlawfully absented himself devouring crops and robbing houses, it is enacted that Billy suffer the pains of death. A reward of a thousand pounds of tobacco is offered for his killing or apprehension. His master is to be paid four thousand pounds of tobacco by the public. A special penalty for harboring, concealing or dealing with Billy is also provided.

1705. Chapter XII.   Masters of ships are not permitted to carry any person, servant or slave out of the country without a license or pass under penalty.

1705. Chapter XXIII.   All Negro, mulatto, and Indian slaves within this dominion shall be held to be real estate and not chattels and shall descend unto heirs and widows according to the custom of land inheritance, and be held in fee simple. Provided that any merchant bringing slaves into this dominion shall hold such slaves whilst they remain unsold as personal estate. All such slaves may be taken on execution as other chattels; slaves shall not be escheatable.

No person selling any slave shall be obliged to have the sale recorded as upon the alienation of other real estate. Nothing in this act shall be construed to give the owner of a slave not seized of other real estate the right to vote as a freeholder.

A widow holding slaves as dower and permitting them or their children to leave the state forfeits every such slave and all other dower.

1705. Chapter XLIX.   This is a general act concerning servants and slaves and covers a great many subjects. A number of the sections are given here, and some are summarized elsewhere in this book. Some of the paragraphs cover Negroes only, some refer to runaways and servants generally, some apparently to indentured servants only.

It is enacted that all servants brought into this country without indenture, if Christian and above nineteen years of age, shall serve but five years, and if under nineteen years till they shall become twenty-four years of age and no longer, but all servants imported by land or sea, who were not Christians in their native country, except Turks and Moors and others, who can make proof of their being free in England or any other Christian country before they were shipped, shall be slaves, and as such be here bought and sold notwithstanding conversion to Christianity afterwards. And for a further Christian care and usage of all Christian servants it is enacted that no Negro, mulatto or Indian, although Christian, or Jew, Moor, Mohammedan, or other infidel, shall purchase any Christian servant, except of their own complexion, or such as are declared slaves by this act. If any Negro or infidel shall notwithstanding purchase any Christian white servant, the said servant shall become free, and if any person having such Christian servant shall intermarry with any such Negro, Indian, Jew or other infidel, every Christian white servant of any such person so intermarrying shall become free.

A penalty is provided for bringing in and selling as a slave any person that shall have been a free man in any Christian country, island, or plantation.

Baptism of slaves does not exempt them from bondage, and all children shall be bond or free, according to the condition of their mother.

No slave may go from the plantation and seat of land where such slave shall be appointed to live without a certificate of leave in writing under penalty of twenty lashes on his bare back, well laid on, and so sent home.

It is the duty of the masters and owners of servants to provide wholesome diet, clothing and lodging and not to give immoderate correction, neither shall they at any time whip a white Christian servant naked; the penalty for so whipping is forty shillings to the person injured.

All servants (not being slaves) shall have their complaints received by a justice of the peace, and an order at the discretion of the court may be made as to diet, lodging, clothing, and correction. On a second complaint the servant may be sold at an outcry by the sheriff, and after charges deducted the remainder shall be paid to the owner.

Sick and disabled servants that cannot be sold shall be taken care of by the church wardens.

Contracts of masters with servants are void unless approved by court; sick or lame servants are not to be discharged, upon pretence of freedom, under penalty.

To every imported servant not having yearly wages, certain amounts shall be paid.

A penalty for resisting a master is provided.

A penalty is provided for dealing with servants or slaves, without leave of their owners. When any such person is convicted and does not give sufficient security for good behavior the court shall order thirty-nine lashes, well laid on, upon the bare back.

Servants shall be given twenty lashes in lieu of every 500 pounds of tobacco to be paid by free persons as fines.

Rewards are to be given for taking up runaway servants or slaves. Such runaways are to be conveyed from constable to constable until carried home and lashed not exceeding thirty-nine times. Damages may be recovered if a constable or sheriff permit a runaway to escape. Runaway servants shall repay all expenses. A penalty is fixed for permitting a slave of another to visit on the place above four hours.

In case any slave who has run away does not immediately return home after a proclamation at the door of every church in the county, it shall be lawful for any person whatsoever to kill and destroy such slave by such means as may be thought fit without accusation of any crime. If any runaway slave shall be apprehended it shall be lawful to order such punishment, either by dismembering or any other way not touching his life, as may be thought fit, for reclaiming such incorrigible slave, and terrifying others from like practices.

Slaves shall not go armed under penalty of twenty lashes on the bare back, well laid on.

All horses, cattle, hogs, now belonging, or that hereafter belong to any slave, shall be seized and sold by the church wardens and the profit thereof applied to the use of the poor of the parish.

For every slave killed, under this act, the owner shall be paid by the public.

In the better putting of this act into execution, and that no servants or slaves may have pretence of ignorance, this act shall be published at church doors and court houses.

When a servant's time has expired his freedom shall be recorded-in court. Whosoever shall hire such servant shall take his certificate until the contracted time has expired; a penalty is fixed for harboring or entertaining a servant without a certificate.

1710. Chapter XVI. Whereas a Negro slave named Will, belonging to Robt. Ruffin, of the County of Surry, was signally serviceable in discovering a conspiracy of Negroes for levying war in this colony; for a reward of his fidelity, it is enacted that the said Will is and forever hereafter shall be free and shall continue to be within this colony, if he think fit to continue. The sum of forty pounds sterling shall be paid the said Robt. Ruffin for the price of Will.

1710. Chapter XVII. This act enables Elizabeth Harrison, widow and administratrix of Benjamin Harrison, to sell bonds and slaves of the estates of the said Benjamin for the payment of debts.

1723. Chapter IV. Whereas the laws now in force for the better governing of slaves are found insufficient to restrain their unlawful and tumultuous meetings, it is enacted that if any number of Negroes exceeding five conspire to rebel, they shall suffer death, and be utterly excluded the benefit of clergy.[1]

Children of female mulattoes or Indians, obliged to serve to the age of thirty or thirty-one years, shall serve the master

[1]For an explanation of this phrase see note on page 154, post.

of such mulatto or Indian until they attain the same age the mother was obliged to serve.

No Negro or Indian slave shall be set free upon any pretence whatsoever, except for some meritorious services, to be adjusted by the governor and council, and a license thereupon obtained. If a slave is set free otherwise than as directed, the church wardens are required to take up and sell the individual as a slave by public outcry and the monies shall be applied to the use of the parish.

It is re-enacted that if slaves are found notoriously guilty of going abroad at night or running away and lying out and cannot be reclaimed from such disorderly courses, it shall be lawful to direct every such slave to be punished by dismembering, or any other way not touching life.

1726. Chapter IV. For the encouragement of constables to perform their duty in conducting runaway slaves, they are exempt from the payment of all public, county and parish levies.

Runaway slaves, whose masters are not known, may be hired out by the keeper of the public gaol, with a strong iron collar with the letters "P. G." stamped thereupon.

Because a former law is not found effectual to prevent masters of vessels from clandestinely transporting persons in debt, servants or slaves out of this colony, they are now required to take oath not to do so.

1727. Chapter XI. This act, to explain and amend the act of 1705, states that slaves are to pass as chattels by bargain and sale, gift and will. The slaves of a woman vest absolutely in her husband on marriage.

Infants above eighteen years of age by last will and testament may dispose of their slaves.

No executor or administrator shall sell slaves, except for the payment of debts, and then only when there is insufficient of the personal estate to pay such debts.

It may be very advantageous to estates to establish a method of settling slaves and their increase so that they may descend with lands and tenements; it is enacted that any person by deed or will wherein lands are conveyed, may declare slaves and their increase shall pass as part of the freehold. Slaves annexed to the land are nevertheless liable to execution and sale for the debts of the tenant in tail.

If any person be possessed of slaves which shall be annexed to the land, they shall not be taken in execution for debt so as to bar the widow.

1732. Chapter VI. Stealing a slave is a felony, and the punishment death without benefit of clergy.

1738. Chapter IX. Slaves are not to be taken on execution unless the debt and costs amounts to 10 pounds, or 2,000 pounds of tobacco, provided there be sufficient other goods.

1740. Chapter XV. Certain slaves of Wm. Chamberlayne, late of New Kent County, were directed by his will to be divided into four lots by the Rev. Daniel Taylor, Daniel Parke Curtis, Richard Littlepage and Francis West, and to go to his wife for her life and then to his children as she would think fit. The wife had a posthumous daughter, remarried, and desired to give this child all the slaves. It is enacted that the said thirty-three slaves are vested in certain gentlemen of New Kent for the widow and her husband to enjoy and after the widow's death to the posthumous child.

1748. Chapter II. Negroes having been declared to be real estate in 1705 and afterward this explained by act in 1727 and the acts having been found inconvenient, they are repealed, and for the future all slaves shall be taken to be chattels.[2]

1748. Chapter III. An act for the distribution of intestate estates provides that widows shall have one-third of all slaves and their increase for life.

1748. Chapter V. An act concerning probate of wills and administration of estates re-enacts earlier legislation and provides slaves may be kept on the plantation to care for crops when the owners die between the first of March and the twenty-fifth of December, until December 25th next following, and such slaves or servants as shall be ten years or more shall be delivered up to the parties having a legal right to them, well clothed at the charge of the decedent's estate.

1748. Chapter XIV. This act concerning servants and slaves enacts that all servants, except convicts, imported without indenture, if they be Christian and above nineteen years of age, shall serve five years, and if under nineteen until twenty-four years of age and no longer. All persons imported who were not Christians in their native land, except Turks and Moors, and those who can prove they were free in England or other Christian country before transportation, shall be slaves, and as such be here bought and sold, notwithstanding conversion to Christianity after importation.

---

[2]1751-1752. Chap. II and other acts of 1748 were repealed by the King's proclamation in 1751 and the Assembly so notified in April, 1752. The Assembly protested that so many of the laws as his majesty deemed expedient be re-enacted. In reference to slaves it was stated that it was thought best to reduce them to their natural condition so that they might not at the same time be real estate in some respects, and personal in others, and both in others; nor did the Assembly think it beneficial or convenient to continue the methods of entailing Negroes any longer.

Children are to be bond or free, according to the condition of their mother. The master's duty to servants is to provide for them and not whip any Christian white servant naked without an order. No contracts shall be made between masters and servants unless in court. Servants shall own their own property. Sick and lame servants shall not be discharged; every servant not having wages shall at the end of his service receive ten pounds ten shillings for freedom dues from the master. Negroes, mulattoes or Indians, although Christians, Jews, Moors, Mohemmedans, or other infidels, shall not purchase Christian servants except of their own complexion. If any person having such Christian servant shall marry with a Negro, mulatto, Indian, Jew, Moor, Mohammedan, or other infidel, such servant shall thereupon become free. There shall be penalties for dealing with servants or slaves without the consent of the master or overseer. Servants shall faithfully do their master's just commands under penalty of extension of time of service. In cases of penal laws, where free persons are punishable by fines, servants shall be punished by whipping at the rate of twenty lashes for every five hundred pounds of tobacco. At the expiration of their term, servants shall have certificates of freedom; there shall be a penalty for harboring servants without certificates; runaways who use stolen or forged certificates shall stand in the pillory two hours; there shall be rewards for taking up runaway servants or slaves. Any Negro or other person not declaring the name of his owner shall be committed to jail and delivered to his owner on satisfying the sheriff's fees; if no owner appear, the runaway shall be hired out, the runaway to wear a strong iron collar with letters "P. G." stamped thereon; owners claiming runaway slaves shall make proof of ownership, but if no owner finally appear the sheriff shall sell the runaway at public auction after charges paid; every runaway servant upon whose account any reward shall be paid, after all other time of service shall be expired, shall repay all charges and loss of time. Servants imported as tradesmen or mechanics, who are ignorant to perform such trades or mysteries, shall repay wages or serve further time as just. Stealing any Negro, mulatto, or Indian slave is a felony and those offending shall suffer death without benefit of clergy.[3]

1748. Chapter XXXVIII. The conspiracy of slaves or their insurrection is a felony and the penalty death without benefit of clergy.

It is repeated that incorrigible slaves going abroad at night may be dismembered by court order and if they die no forfeiture nor punishment shall be incurred.

1752. Chapter XLII. Whereas the breed of sheep is greatly diminished in many parts of this dominion by reason that Negroes and other slaves are not restrained from carrying dogs about with them; for the prevention thereof, it is enacted that it shall not be lawful for any Negro or other slave in going from one plantation to another to carry any dog whatsoever, under penalty of having the dog killed and twenty lashes on the bare back. But nothing herein shall hinder any person from sending his slave from place to place with his hounds, spaniels, pointers, or setting dogs, for his diversion.

1753. Chapter VII. An act for the better government of servants and slaves re-enacts much of Chapter XIV, 1748, with

---

[3]Some of the paragraphs of this and similar laws deal with both servants and slaves; some with servants only, others with slaves only.

sections on the bastard children of women servants by free
fathers, by Negroes, or mulattoes, the intermarriage of whites
and Negroes, etc.[4]

1757. Chapter VI. Whereas many frauds have been committed by secret gifts of slaves, whereby creditors have been
deprived of their just debts, gifts of slaves hereafter must be
by will, deed or testament, proved by two witnesses at least,
in writing and recorded.

1765. Chapter XXIV. Whereas divers ill-disposed persons
have been guilty of selling certain mulattoes and others as
slaves, who are by law subject to serve only to thirty-one
years of age, after which they become free, it is enacted that
any one so doing knowingly shall forfeit fifty pounds to the
purchaser. If any person shall be guilty a second time of selling the same servant as a slave, he shall forfeit the residue of
the time due from such servant, who shall thereupon be
bound to serve until twenty-one years of age, in the same manner as is directed for orphan children. If the person selling
cannot pay this fine, he must serve the buyer the time that
would have been due from the servant.

1765. Chapter XXV. This law for the better government
of slaves and servants enacts that runaway slaves and servants may be carried by the taker-up to the owner; the taker-
up shall be entitled to five shillings for taking up, and four
pence for every mile covered.

1769. Chapter XIX. The taker-up of a runaway at his option may convey him to his owner, or if the owner is not in
the county, carry him to gaol, and the gaoler shall advertise

[4]See Chapter I.

a description of the runaway in the *Virginia Gazette* for three weeks.

Whereas many owners of slaves in consideration of wages to be paid by such slaves license them to go at large, to trade as free men, which is a great encouragement to theft and other evil practices by the slaves, in order to enable them to fulfill their agreements with their owners; it is enacted that if any owner license a slave to trade as a free man, he shall forfeit the sum of ten pounds in current money for the use of the poor of the parish, to be recovered by the church wardens.

1772. Chapter XIX. Vessels importing convicts, indented servants, and slaves, infected with the gaol fever or small pox shall perform quarantine under penalties and forfeiture.[5]

1776. A Declaration of Rights unanimously adopted by the Virginia Assembly at Williamsburg, June 12, declares in its first paragraph all men are by nature free and independent, and have certain inherent rights, namely, the enjoyment of life and liberty, with the means of acquiring property, and obtaining happiness and safety. In the last paragraph it is stated all men are equally entitled to the free exercise of religion according to the dictates of conscience, and it is the mutual duty of all to practice Christian forbearance, love and charity toward each other.

1776. On June 19, the Virginia Constitution was adopted and recites in its preamble as a grievance against George III that he prompted the Negroes to rise in arms, those very

---

[5] Amends similar legislation of 1766 and before.

Negroes whom, by an inhuman use of his negative, he had refused permission to exclude by law.

1776. Chapter XXVI. Any person who has any estate in lands or slaves in tail is to hold in fee simple, under named conditions.

1778. Chapter I. In the third year of the Commonwealth, Patrick Henry, Esquire, being Governor, at the Capitol at Williamsburg, it is enacted, that hereafter no slave shall be imported into the Commonwealth by sea or land. Every slave imported contrary to the interest and meaning of this act shall become free.

Provided that persons may remove from any of the United States to Virginia if not with the intention of evading this act, and their slaves were not imported from Africa or any of the West Indies since November 1, 1778.

1779. Chapter XLIV. A Negro slave named Kitt, owned by Hinchia Mabry, of Brunswick, has rendered meritorious service in making the first information against several counterfeiters, and is hereby emancipated and his owner ordered paid 1,000 pounds out of the public treasury.

1779. Chapter XLVII. Application has been made to the General Assembly that John Hope (called Barber Caesar), Wm. Beck and a mulatto girl, Peg, be emancipated. They are hereby declared free and may enjoy all the rights which free Negroes by the laws of this country enjoy, with a saving to all persons (except the present owners), any claim they may have to the said Negroes.[6]

---

[6] In 1780, two others were similarly emancipated.

1780. Chapter XXXIII. Citizens of South Carolina and Georgia, who are compelled by the common enemy to fly the country and seek shelter in this Commonwealth, may in spite of the former law bring their slaves into this state and may continue the slaves here until one year after the expulsion of the enemy from the state from which the slaves came. If they remain longer than a year, they shall become free, except such slaves as are sold by the owner for his necessary support.

1782. Chapter XXI. It is lawful for any person by last will and testament or other instrument in writing sealed and witnessed to emancipate and set free his slave or slaves.

All slaves so set free, not being of sound mind and body, or being above forty-five years of age, or males under twenty-one, and females under eighteen shall be supported by the persons liberating them. Provided, also, that a copy of the instrument of emancipation shall be delivered to the slave emancipated. Slaves travelling outside of the county without such an instrument may be confined to jail.

1782. Chapter. XXXII. Because great inconvenience has arisen from persons permitting their slaves to go at large and hire themselves out, under promise of paying their owners money in lieu of services, it is enacted that if slaves are permitted to go at large, they may be sold and disposed of by the sheriff. Twenty-five per cent of the amount of the sale shall go toward lessening the county levy, five per cent to the gaoler and the rest to the owner of the slave.

1782. Chapter XLV. Slaves may be tendered on judgments exceeding twenty pounds and the act is continued in 1783 because of the scarcity of specie and inability of debtors to pay except in produce.

1785. Chapter LXI. An act concerning wills and intestates declares that a widow who removes a slave from the Commonwealth shall forfeit all the slaves she holds, and all other dower. If the husband of a widow removes a slave, the owner in reversion may claim the estate.

If a person die after the first day of March, his servants and slaves shall be continued on the plantation until the last day of December following, and then delivered to those who have a right to them.

1785. Chapter LXXVII. No person shall henceforth be a slave in Virginia, except such as were so on the first day of this Assembly and the descendants of the females of them. Slaves hereafter brought in and kept one year shall be free.

A slave shall not go from where he lives without a license or letter showing he has authority from his master.

Slaves shall not keep arms; riots and unlawful assemblies by slaves shall be punished by stripes.

It is provided that persons who wish to move into this Commonwealth may take oath that their removal was not with intent to evade laws preventing the importation of slaves, that the slaves are not to be sold, nor have they been bought since November 1, 1778.

A penalty is provided for dealing with slaves without the consent of the owner.

1785. Chapter LXXXIII. An act concerning servants states all white persons not being citizens of any of the confederated states of America, who shall come into this Commonwealth under contract to serve another, shall be compelled to perform such contract as shall not exceed seven years. Infants under fourteen years shall serve until twenty-one or for such shorter term as is fixed. Servants shall be provided by their master with food, clothes, lodging; lazy, disorderly servants may, on order of a justice, be corrected by stripes, and serve two days for every day they refuse to serve. If the master fail in his duties to his servants, they may be discharged from service if the injury is gross. All contracts between master and servant are void.

1785. Chapter LXXXIV. Runaway servants and slaves may be apprehended by any person, who shall be rewarded by the owner. If the owner is not found, the runaway shall be placed in jail, and may be hired out with an iron collar on his neck. A runaway being a slave, after one year from the last advertisement in the *Virginia Gazette,* shall be sold.

1787. Chapter XXII. This act, in reference to fraudulent gifts of slaves, states that the former act was not to refer to slaves, except those which remain in the possession of donors after being given away.

1787. Chapter LXXIII. The will of Joseph Mayo, of Henrico County, freeing his slaves is confirmed and his benevolent intentions given effect.

1787. Chapter LXXIV. Also certain slaves of Charles Moorman, of Louisa County, are given freedom by legislative act confirming their owner's intentions.

1788. Chapter XII. A practice has prevailed for some time past of importing felons convict into this state under various pretenses, which felons convict have been sold among the people, whereby much injury has been done to the morals as well as the health of the citizens; therefore, it is enacted that after January 1 next no such shall be imported under penalty.

1788. Chapter LIV. Many persons have removed into Kentucky and have failed to take their oaths as required on importing slaves, it is now provided that they may take their oaths on or before May 1, 1789.

1789. Chapter XLV. Persons migrating into Virginia with their slaves, who have not taken the oath, may take it on or before June 1, 1790.[7]

1790. Chapter XIII. When an equal division of the slaves of an intestate cannot be made, they may be sold and the money distributed.

1792. Chapter 41. This is an act to reduce into one the several acts concerning slaves, free Negroes, and mulattoes, and it says that slaves shall be those who were such on October 17, 1785, and the descendants of the females of them. Slaves brought in and kept one year shall be free, with an exception for owners who take the oath formerly required.

Slaves coming on to a plantation without their owner's leave may be given ten lashes on their bare backs by the owner or overseer of such plantation.

Negroes and mulattoes shall not carry guns, except free Negroes may be permitted to keep one gun, and Negroes, bond or free, living on the frontier may be licensed to keep them.

---

[7] It was declared in 1790 that the oath could be taken on or before October 1, 1791.

Whereas slaves run away and hide out and kill hogs, it is enacted that upon intelligence of two or more lying out, they may be committed to jail for trial.

Conspiracy to rebel, or make insurrection, is deemed a felony, with death the punishment without benefit of clergy.

Slaves may be emancipated by an instrument in writing, attested and proved by two witnesses; provided they shall be liable to be taken on execution to satisfy any debt contracted previously by the person so emancipating. Slaves not being of sound mind and body, or between eighteen years of age, if female, and twenty-one years of age, if male, and forty-five years shall be supported by the person liberating them. The property of the former master may be distrained and sold for this purpose.[8]

All Negroes and mulattoes are adjudged personal estate.[9]

Widows are not to remove slaves from the state or forfeit them and the rest of their dower.

If the donor remains in possession of a slave, a gift of a slave is not valid.

Slaves are not to prepare or administer medicine with provisoes.

Slaves are not to trade as free men under penalty of $30.00 for each offense.[10]

1792. Chapter 67. All white persons not being citizens of any of the confederated states of America, who shall come in under contract to serve another, shall be compellable to perform such contract during the term thereof or during so much of the same as shall not exceed seven years. Infants un-

---

[8]The law on emancipation was substantially the same in 1860.
[9]Slaves were deemed personal estate by successive acts to the Civil War, but see Chap. 34, 1828, Chapter IV, post.
[10]This penalty was increased to $40.00 in 1801.

der fourteen shall serve to twenty-one years or for such shorter term as their contract fixes.

It is the master's duty to provide servants with food, clothing, etc.

Lazy, disorderly servants shall be corrected with stripes on order from a justice. The servant shall be compelled to serve two days for every one he refuses to serve.

Courts may discharge servants from service if masters injure them grossly. Contracts between master and servant during the time of service shall be void. Courts shall receive complaints of servants who allege immoderate correction, insufficient food, etc., and complaints of masters against their servants.

A servant who is lazy, disorderly, or guilty of misbehavior to his master shall be corrected by stripes.

No Negro, mulatto, or Indian shall purchase any servant other than of their own complexion, and if any of the aforesaid persons do purchase a white servant such servant shall immediately become free. Servants when free shall have certificates thereof.

No person shall buy of or sell to any servant any commodity without the leave or consent of the master or owner of such servant under penalty of forfeiting four times the value of the thing bought or sold, and also forfeit $20.00 or receive on his or her bare back thirty-nine lashes, well laid on at the public whipping post.

1792. Chapter 72. If any person on a Sabbath day is found laboring, or shall employ his apprentices, servants, or slaves in labor or other business, except in household offices of daily necessity, or other work of necessity or charity, he shall forfeit the sum of $1.67 for every such offense; the punishment for profane swearing, cursing and drunkenness is set in this act at 83 cents for every such offense, and for the adultery and fornication of every person not a servant or slave $20.00 and $10.00, respectively.

1793. Chapter 3. Slaves shall not be seized in execution unless the debt amounts to $33.00 or 2,000 pounds of tobacco if there is sufficient other goods upon which the levy may be made.

Slaves, horses and livestock taken in execution shall be supported until sold.

1794. Chapter 19. Whereas doubts may arise whether slaves being personal estate are perishable and liable through age or sickness to be rendered less valuable by keeping, executors and administrators are bound to sell the same whether it be necessary for the payment of debts or not. For declaring the law, it is further enacted that slaves shall not be sold unless the other part of the personal estate shall not be sufficient for paying the debts and expenses.

1795. Chapter II. Whereas great and alarming mischief has arisen in other states of this Union, and is likely to arise in this by voluntary association of individuals, who under cover of effecting that justice toward persons unwarrantably held in slavery, which the sovereignty and duty of society alone ought to afford; have in many instances been the means of depriving masters of their property in slaves: To the end that an easy mode may be pointed out by law for the recovery of freedom when it is illegally denied, it is enacted that a person conceiving himself to be detained as a slave illegally may make complaint in court; the petitioner shall be assigned counsel who without fee shall prosecute the suit.[11]

If any person aid or abet any person in such a claim for freedom and the claim is not established, he shall forfeit one hundred dollars to the owner of the slave.

A widow who renounces all benefit under her husband's will shall be entitled to one-third part of her husband's slaves, notwithstanding they may be emancipated by his will; provided, nevertheless, that her part shall be taken out of slaves which are not emancipated if there be enough to make one-third.

A person forging or counterfeiting a paper giving a slave freedom shall pay two hundred dollars and suffer one year's imprisonment without bail.

1796. Chapter II. If slaves are carried from this state by their owners, they may be brought back to Virginia, and they are not entitled to their freedom, unless they are entitled to their freedom under the laws of that other state.

1796. Chapter 43. This act authorizes the Potomac Company to employ at the great falls of the Potomac River slaves from Maryland, not exceeding fifty for one year.

1798. Chapter 4. Free persons conspiring with slaves to rebel shall suffer death. Free persons harboring or entertaining any slave without the master's consent shall pay ten dollars, free Negroes not able to pay shall receive not to exceed thirty-nine lashes.

---

[11]The courts held there was a legal presumption that a person who appeared to be a Negro was a slave.

It is further enacted that in cases wherein the property of a person held as a slave demanding freedom shall come for trial, no person shall serve as a juror who shall belong to a society for the emancipation of Negroes.

It is made a felony for a free Negro to give his certificate of freedom to a slave. The skipper of a vessel must not carry a slave out of the state until he has taken him before a magistrate, and made out a description of the slave and shall have produced the slave's certificate of freedom.[12]

---

[12]In 1802 an additional penalty was placed on skippers who permitted slaves to come on board, in case the skipper himself was a slave he was to receive thirty-nine lashes on the bare back.

In 1805, another penalty of two hundred dollars was added for skippers who allowed slaves aboard their vessels, one-third to the masters, one-third to the informer, and one-third to the overseer for the use of the poor.

CHAPTER IV

Slaves in the Eighteen Hundreds

1801. Chapter 34. Sound policy dictates that rewards should be held out to those who have rendered essential service to our country, the governor is therefore authorized to purchase and set free Pharoah, slave of Philip Sheppard, and Tom, slave of Elizabeth Sheppard.

1801. Chapter 43. Slaves under sentence of death for conspiracy, insurrection or other crime may be purchased by the governor and transported. The owners of all slaves sold or transported shall be paid in the same manner as for slaves executed.[1]

1801. Chapter 70. If any person permits his slave, or any slave hired by him, to go at large or hire himself out, the slave may be sold.[2] It is enacted that if any slave shall be brought or come into this state from any place without the limits of the state, it shall be the duty of any magistrate where such slave is found to commit the slave to jail, and the magistrate shall notify the governor and the slave shall be transported out of the Commonwealth and the expenses incurred shall be paid by the person importing or holding the slave, but the slave may be sold within the Commonwealth

---

[1] The law giving the owner of a slave condemned to die the value of the slave even though he perished or escaped or was sold for transportation continued in effect until the Civil War.

[2] This law was several times amended. In the Code of 1860 it was declared that any person permitting a slave under his control to go at large and trade as a free man, or hire himself out should forfeit $10.00-$30.00.

if the person holding him is unable to reimburse the Commonwealth.

1802. Chapter 21. An additional penalty is placed on any person who buys from or sells to a free Negro or slave any commodity whatever on the Sabbath day, without leave in writing from the master.

1804. Chapter 89. When slaves are held by widows or others for life they shall be registered, with the ages, sexes, and increase of such slaves.

1804. Chapter 97. It is lawful for any citizen of the Commonwealth or of the County of Alexandria in the District of Columbia, who has carried or may carry slaves into the county in the district aforesaid, owning lands within this state, to remove the slaves back to Virginia, without penalty, and the slaves shall not be entitled to freedom on that account.

1804. Chapter 119. All meetings of slaves at any meeting house or any other place in the night shall be considered an unlawful assembly, and any justice may issue his warrant to enter the place where the assembly may be for apprehending or dispersing the slaves, and to inflict corporal punishment on the offenders at the discretion of the justice, not exceeding twenty lashes.[a]

Any person may be summoned to aid in the execution of this act and may be fined not exceeding $10.00 for refusing to serve; counties west of the Blue Ridge are excepted from this act.

1805. By resolution the General Assembly of Virginia, on January 31, votes not to endorse the amendment to the United

[a]See 1832, Chap. XXII, Free Persons of Color and Slaves for later and fuller statement on religious meetings.

States Constitution proposed by the state of North Carolina which would forbid the further importation of slaves. The reason assigned by Virginia is that such an amendment would violate the United States Constitution that no such amendment be adopted prior to 1808.

1805. Chapter 11.   Carrying away any slave is a misdemeanor, punishable by a fine of from $100.00 to $500.00 and imprisonment in the jail or penitentiary from two to four years, and payment to the owner of the slave of double the value of the slave.

Masters of vessels who permit slaves to come on board, or who buy any commodity from a slave without consent of the owner, shall forfeit $200.00 in addition to the penalties now imposed.

1805. Chapter 12.   It is declared that it is not unlawful for masters to permit slaves to accompany them, or any part of the family to religious worship if it is conducted by a white minister.

1806. Chapter 63.   Slaves brought into this state and kept one year shall be forfeited by the owner, and the right to the slaves shall rest in the overseers of the poor, who shall apprehend such slaves for the benefit of the poor.

If any slave hereafter emancipated shall remain within this Commonwealth more than twelve months after his freedom, he shall forfeit such right, and may be sold by the overseers for the benefit of the poor.[4]

---

[4]Later the proceeds of such sales went to the Literary Fund, and courts on proof of the extraordinary merit of an applicant could permit a slave emancipated for extraordinary merit since May 1, 1806, to remain, and also his emancipated wife, husband or children on proof of their good character and conduct. Rejections of applications to remain were final, and leaves to remain were forfeited on conviction of an offense. See Code 1819, Chap. III also Chapter V post Free Persons of Color and Slaves.

1807. Chapter 12. Persons leaving the state with the intention of returning may bring back their slaves. Persons, inhabitants of this state on January 25, 1806, shall have also the right to bring into this state within six months any slaves, and their increase since that day, whereof they were and are the real owners. Inhabitants of other states may employ their slaves in bringing produce into this state.

1808. Chapter 15. Any person who may hereafter apprehend a runaway slave shall be entitled to a reward of $2.00, and mileage as heretofore. If the owner does not claim a runaway within twelve months, the sheriff shall advertise for one month in any public newspaper the time and place of selling the runaway.

1809. Chapters XCV & XCVIII. James Stephenson, of Berkeley County, is given permission to bring a Negro girl into the state, the law to the contrary notwithstanding. Also John H. Winder is given similar permission.

1810. Chapter LXXIII. It appears that George Simmons, a man of color, is held in bondage by Travers Daniel, of Stafford County, who purchased him at the particular request of the said George's reputed father, a white man and a citizen of the Commonwealth. It was intended that George be emancipated as soon as Daniel had been reimbursed the purchase money. Daniel has acknowledged he has been reimbursed and desires George to be emancipated with the privilege of remaining within the state. It is ordered that George Simmons be permitted to remain in the state if emancipated by Daniel.

1810. Chapter LXXIV. One John Mitchell, late of Maryland, whose house there burned, is permitted to return and reside in the state of Virginia and bring with him his two female slaves, without penalty, any law to the contrary notwithstanding.

1810. Chapter LXXV. John S. Smith, of Prince William County, is permitted to hold a certain slave, who had previously run away from Maryland but has been recovered.

1810. Chapter LXXX. Polly Coleman is permitted to hold a Negro named Hannah who had been carried to Georgia.

1810. Chapter LXXXVII. John Read is also permitted to bring in a group of slaves who had been taken to North Carolina.

1810. Chapter LXXXIX. Parmelia Burrus is permitted to bring certain slaves in from Tennessee.[5]

1811. Chapter XIV. Inconveniences arising in the law on slaves, it is amended and herewith provided that persons, citizens of this Commonwealth and residing therein, who now are or may hereafter be entitled by marriage, descent, or devise, to any slave in any other of the United States, shall be at liberty to bring them into this state, provided a certificate within sixty days is filed from the court of the place from which the slaves come showing how the slaves were required and a description of their persons and names.

1812. Chapter XXVI. Persons residing in this state or removing here, owners of slaves born in United States, are permitted to bring them in, provided in thirty days a statement

---

[5]During the same year there were many similar permissions.

in writing giving a description of the slaves and a true account of the slaves brought is filed, and the slaves were not brought in for the purpose of sale or with intent to evade the laws preventing importation of slaves, and provided also if female slaves, ten to thirty years of age, are exported within three months, a report shall be made to the court. It is further enacted that persons who have brought slaves in contrary to the law of 1806 concerning slaves shall be permitted to retain such slaves.

1812. Chapter CXIV. The fine and forfeiture incurred by Solomon Betton, of Loudoun County, for bringing in a slave, named Tom, contrary to law are remitted on condition that the slave be removed in sixty days.

1812. Chapter CXXVII. Richard Walker is permitted to bring in from Tennessee four slaves who are particularly valuable to him, any law notwithstanding.

1812. Chapter CXXXIV. Certain slaves which were carried to Illinois are now permitted to be returned to Virginia.

1813. Chapter XVIII. A citizen of the Commonwealth owner of any slave out of the Commonwealth born in the United States, and any person removing here with the intention to become a bona fide inhabitant and owner of any slave for two years, or having acquired title by marriage, descent, or devise, are authorized to bring into the state any such slaves, provided that within sixty days they file certain written statements. Penalties are remitted on citizens who have brought slaves in contrary to law, provided that they file the statements required. Slaves brought in under this act are not to be sold for two years.

1813. Chapter CXXXV. The Auditor of Public Accounts is required to issue a warrant in favor of William Gaines for the sum of money from the sale of a Negro man purchased by Gaines from an inhabitant of North Carolina, whence the said Negro was brought in 1812 and sold in consequence by the overseers of the poor.

1814. Chapter C. James Forsee is permitted to hold a slave brought in from Kentucky, although from ignorance he omitted to make the statements and procure the certificate required.

1814. Chapter CI. One John Griffith is allowed to hold as his property in this state a slave named Molly, imported from Maryland, which was derived by descent by the said Griffith from his father.

1814. Chapter CII. In January Richard M. Scott is authorized to bring in thirteen slaves.

In November Mary Andrews, of Williamsburg, is permitted to bring in certain slaves, which were loaned to her by gentlemen from the Mississippi Territory.[6]

1814. Chapter CIII. In January Philip Smith and Charles Burks are permitted to hold certain slaves brought in.

In November Wm. Trimble is permitted to hold a slave, Abraham, from Kentucky, a justice of the peace having failed to make out the required certificate.[6]

1814. Chapter CIV. Also in December Wm. Hogan is permitted to hold his slaves, imported from Kentucky, without forfeitures.[7]

[6]The year and the act numbers are the same here but the sessions different.
[7]There were many similar acts in reference to other slaves at this period.

1817. Chapter XV. If any free person advise or conspire with any other free person or Negro to induce or excite any slave to rebel or make insurrection, every such free person shall be held a felon and suffer death by hanging.[*]

1817. Chapter XXI. Any person removing into the Commonwealth with the intention of becoming a citizen and inhabitant and being the owner of any slaves born within the United States may bring such slaves in, in the same manner as if at the time of such removel he had been the owner thereof for two years (subject to other provisions of the act of 1813). A provision is here added in favor of persons who have removed to this Commonwealth since January, 1813, freeing them of penalties as if they had been the owners of slaves for two years. Persons owning lands in Virginia, and in any adjoining state or the District of Columbia, may lawfully work their slaves in any one or all such farms, but such slaves are not to be sold in this Commonwealth.

Persons living in this Commonwealth may hire their slaves out to other states or hire slaves from other states for one or two years, but the children of female slaves cannot remain beyond the continuance of the hiring. Slaves acquired by gift may be brought in on the same conditions as if acquired by marriage, descent, or devise.

1817. Chapter XXXVI. Because of serious inconvenience experienced by Virginians from the frequent elopement of slaves to states north of the Potomac it is enacted that hereafter $20.00 reward, and mileage, be allowed any person who may apprehend any runaway slave attempting to cross the Potomac if the plantation on which the slave is employed be

---

[*]See 1832, Chap. XXII, Free Persons of Color on this subject.

not less than ten miles from the river. If the slave is apprehended in Maryland or Kentucky, the reward shall be $25.00; in Delaware, New Jersey, Pennsylvania, New York, or Ohio, $50.00, plus twenty-five cents a mile.

Keepers of bridges and ferries must not permit slaves to cross the river without special permits. Runaway slaves committed to jail shall be advertised in a Richmond newspaper.

1818. Chapter CLXX. One Jeremiah Franklin is permitted to hold in Virginia a Negro boy from North Carolina named Wesley, given to Franklin by his father, but the slave is not to be sold within two years.

1818. Chapter CLXXXIX. Two slaves brought in from Georgia may be held by their owners.

1818. Chapter CXCII. One Marmaduke Ganneway is authorized to bring in a slave, a carpenter from Tennessee, that he got in exchange for one of bad character.[9]

1818. Chapter CXCVIII. William Givins is permitted to keep a Negro girl who was brought in from Tennessee some years ago, without penalty, because at the time of the removal he was entirely ignorant of the laws in relation to the importation of slaves.

1818. Chapter CC. George Whitlocke, of Lynchburg, is permitted to bring in a Negro boy, Edmund, from Kentucky who had been left behind for punishment for some misconduct.

---

[9]Many other special laws are found at this time permitting owners to hold slaves brought in from other states for a variety of reasons. Slaves, the husbands or wives of other slaves who were already in Virginia, were sometimes permitted to remain.

1818. Chapter CCIV. The sum of $400.00 is ordered to be paid the owner of a Negro slave, Hercules, who was condemned to death for burglary but broke jail and escaped.

1819. Chapter XXVI. This is an act concerning slaves and free Negroes and states that no persons shall be slaves within this Commonwealth, except such as were so on October 17, 1785, and the descendants of the females, and such slaves as since have been, or may be brought in pursuant to law. It shall be lawful to bring into this state and hold therein any slave born within the United States, except such as at the time of their removal were resident out of the United States, and such as shall have been convicted of any offense and transported therefor, under the laws of this state, or of any other state. A penalty for the use of the Literary Fund, for bringing in slaves not permitted by law is set at $1,000.00 for each slave, with an exception for those passing through the state, or abiding in the state for a short time, if the slaves are not kept here for a whole year. Penalties heretofore incurred are remitted.

1819. Chapter CXLII. This act authorizes the commissioners to sell the land and a woman slave and her five children, which belong to one Lucy Bullock, a lunatic.

1819. Chapter CLIX. Frances D. Tucker brought with her an attendant, a female slave, Sally, from Bermuda, understanding she could legally retain the said slave twelve months within the Commonwealth. Before that time she sent the slave to North Carolina, but sustains considerable inconvenience on account of the loss of her services. For remedy, it is enacted that Frances D. Tucker may introduce and retain within the Commonwealth, the female slave, Sally.

1819. Chapter CLXXI. Thomas Woodford is permitted to bring back from Kentucky twelve slaves, together with their increase, a family misfortune having since destroyed the motive which induced him to meditate removal.

1819. Chapter CLXXII. Perryn Cardwell, ignorant of the act of the legislature, is permitted to hold eight slaves brought from North Carolina in 1816 free from fines.

1819. Chapter CLXXIII. Henry Hines, totally ignorant of the fact that he is required to have certificates of exportation and importation of slaves certified and recorded within a certain period, is permitted to hold Hannah, a slave, free from fine or forfeiture in this Commonwealth.

1819. Chapter CLXXIV. Henry Dupree is authorized to hold eight slaves brought in from North Carolina.

1819. Chapter CLXXV. A widow, Polly B. Glover, is authorized to hold six slaves brought in from Alabama, on whose labor she and her infant child depend solely for support.

1819. Chapter CLXXVI. Richard P. Montgomery is authorized to hold three slaves brought in from North Carolina.

1819. Chapter CLXXVII. A similar act is passed for Thomas Byrd concerning one slave from Kentucky.

1819. Chapter CLXXVIII. James Caldwell is authorized to hold four slaves from Maryland because at the time of removal he was entirely ignorant of the laws on the importation of slaves.

1819. Chapter CLXXIX. One Lewis Webb, of Richmond, is authorized to hold three slaves acquired by marriage in North Carolina and removed to this state last year.

1819. Chapter CLXXXI. A certain slave, John, property of John Thornton, of Caroline County, was convicted of murder, and sentenced, but members of the bar and many other respectable citizens petitioned the executive either to transport him, or to pardon him. The pardon was granted after the prisoner escaped. The sum of $800.00 is ordered paid Thornton. If the slave is hereafter apprehended, he shall be sold by the sheriff and the proceeds paid into the public treasury.

1820. Chapter 116. The sum of $600.00 is allowed William Walker as indemnification for a slave condemned to die who broke jail and escaped after the change of his sentence to transportation.

1820. Chapter CXXX. Julia Berkeley, widow of Dr. Robt. Berkeley, of Frederick, who was murdered under circumstances of frightful and appalling barbarity, is authorized to sell the slaves who have not been executed because no one is willing to hire them for a reasonable price.

1820. Chapter CXLIII. An order for William Bosher, owner of a slave under death sentence who broke jail, is made for $800.00.

1822. Chapter 22. Runaway slaves confined in jail hereafter are not to be sold by the sheriff, except on court order.

1823. Chapter 30. Whenever a runaway slave is confined in jail and is not provided with adequate clothing, it shall be the duty of the jailor to furnish him with proper Negro clothing or other necessaries.

1823. Chapter 35. The reward for apprehending runaway slaves in Ohio, Pennsylvania, or Indiana, shall be $50.00 and 20 cents per mile for traveling to the residence of the owner or the jail at which the runaway is delivered. The reward shall be $120.00 for apprehending slaves in New York, New England, and the British Provinces. The rewards allowed shall operate as a lien on the slave. If the slave is taken up not more than twenty miles distant from his plantation, the reward shall be $25.00 and mileage.

1823. Chapter 102. A slave of William Tompkins was committed as a free man of color to the penitentiary for fifteen years. It is now enacted that he be sold and the sum paid his owner and he be transported.

1824. Chapter 34. Sam, a Negro man, slave of Robt. Ricks, condemned to death and his valuation paid his owner, escaped and has been retaken; it is here ordered he be sold and transported beyond the limits of the Commonwealth. It is further enacted that the owners of old slaves, or slaves of unsound mind who permit them to go at large without support, so that they are dependent on charity, trespass, or theft shall pay a fine of not exceeding $50.00 for every offense, and it moreover shall be the duty of the overseers of the poor to provide for such slaves and charge the master.

1824. Chapter 35. For enticing or advising any servant or slave away from home, or knowingly employing or harboring a runaway servant or slave, the penalty is $10.00 to $20.00, one-half to the informer and the other half to the Literary Fund, or ten to twenty lashes on the bare back if not paid.[19] Search warrants are to be allowed to search for runaway slaves. Whenever the master or owner of any slave shall desire to confine him in jail, it shall be lawful for the jailer to receive him, provided the justice be of the opinion he may be confined without public inconvenience, and he shall not be confined in the same apartment with any free white person.

1824. Chapter 36. The jailer of Prince William County is allowed certain sums for keping runaway slaves and it is further enacted that hereafter jailers are to report to courts confined runaway slaves within two months. Three disinterested persons shall then value the slave, and if the court be of the opinion that the runaway will not sell at auction for sufficient to pay the prison fees after being confined twelve months, they shall fix the time of imprisonment for a shorter period and order the slave sold.

1823. Chapter 34. In an act concerning guardians, orphans, and infants it is stated that slaves acquired by an infant are to descend as real estate in the event of the death of an infant under age.

1828. Chapter 166. One Alice E. Farley, a widow who owns a life estate in a few slaves, is permitted to remove them from the state without the consent of the reversioners, who being infants are incapable of giving it.

1829. Chapter 21. Persons assisting slaves to escape are guilty of a misdemeanor and shall be punished by confinement in jail three to twelve months, be fined at the discretion of the jury, and liable also to action by the party aggrieved.

---

[19]It is interesting to note this section refers to servants as well as slaves.

Jailors shall try to ascertain the owners of runaway slaves and notify them by mail.

1829. Chapter 175. This act authorizes a widow and an administrator to sell certain slaves of one Solomon Jacobs, deceased, of Richmond, the proceeds to be put into stock to be held under the same terms as the slaves.

1829. Chapter 176. This act authorizes the sale by his committee of the slaves of Thomas G. Pollard, a lunatic confined in the hospital at Williamsburg.

1830. Chapter 17. Certificates are to be obtained by slave owners who are about to remove slaves to Louisiana signed by two freeholders, stating that the slaves were raised by the present owners, or acquired in a named county and have not been convicted of any crimes.

1835. Chapter 62. If the owner of a runaway slave does not claim him within four months after the keeper of the jail has advertised, the runaway shall be sold.

1835. Chapter 149. This act incorporates the Virginia Slave Insurance Company, with power and authority to make insurance upon slaves absconding from their owners.

1836. Chapter 73. The head man of each boat navigating rivers and branches shall keep a list of the crew, and if any slave not belonging to the boat, nor in the list of the crew, be found on board without the leave of his master, he shall be deemed a runaway. The head man of the boat, if white, shall be liable to a penalty of $20.00, to be paid the owner of the runaway; if the head man be a slave or free Negro, he shall be whipped not exceeding thirty-nine lashes on his bare back, but in the case of a free Negro he may discharge himself by paying as in the case of a white man. Free Negroes employed on boats shall carry their freedom papers and be committed to jail if found without them and dealt with as runaways.

1836. Chapter 90. If any pilot aprehends and confines in jail any runaway slave found on board a departing vessel, he shall be entitled to a reward of $20.00, to be recovered from the owner. And, moreover, the master, skipper or owner of the vessel in which the slave may be found shall forfeit the sum of $500.00 in addition to the penalties now prescribed by law.

1837. Chapter 117. Railroads are forbidden to receive any slave or slaves on cars, without first obtaining permission in writing from the owner under penalty of $100.00, one-half to the use of the Literary Fund and one-half to the use of the party aggrieved, and shall be moreover liable to the party aggrieved, for damages.

1837. Chapter 334. This act permits Elizabeth Anderson, of Nottoway County, to remove from the Commonwealth certain slaves held by her under the will of her husband.

1837. Chapter 335. Lewis Smith and his wife, Emeline, who are possessed of a life estate in certain personal property consisting of slaves, held by right of dower, in the estate of her former husband, are authorized to remove the slaves from the Commonwealth to Mississippi.

1838. Chapter 296. This act authorizes Sarah W. Harper to remove seven dower slaves beyond the limits of the

Commonwealth into the state of Missouri, or elsewhere within the United States, one of the slave men valued at fifty dollars less than nothing.

1838. Chapter 297. The sale of certain personal estate consisting of slaves, some of whom are quite young, and others much advanced in life, is authorized, the proceeds to be paid to the guardian of the owners.

1839. Chapter 76. It is declared a felony to permit slaves to cross ferries or bridges without their owners' consent in writing, punishment two to five years and liability also to private action.

1840. Chapter 61. A slave condemned to be hung or transported shall be valued by each justice at the cash price for which he would sell at public sale under a knowledge of his guilt. From such valuation the court shall ascertain the average value of the slave, and such average shall be paid to the owner by the Commonwealth.

It shall be lawful to commute the punishment of transportation and sale to imprisonment of five to ten years as if the person were free. Persons whose sentences have been commuted shall within thirty days after the expiration of their terms depart from the state, or be dealt with as free persons migrating into the Commonwealth contrary to law.

1841. Chapter 73. Any person apprehending a runaway slave above sixteen years of age more than twenty miles from his place of abode and within ten miles of dividing lines between Ohio, Pennsylvania, and Maryland shall be entitled to recover $30.00 and ten cents for every mile he shall necessarily convey the runaway.

1841. Chapter 159. An act for the relief of Bryan Lester, of Mecklenburg County, authorizes the payment of $500.00 in his favor for a certain condemned slave.

1843. Chapter 101. The Rivanna Navigation Company is hereby authorized to purchase, hold and dispose of as many slaves as may be necessary to the uses of the company.

1843. Chapter 159. This act authorizes the removal of certain slaves held for life under a will, to Maryland, without incurring the penalty.

1843. Chapter 164. One Meriwether, of Albemarle County, is allowed $500.00 for a condemned slave, and one Wilson, of Fauquier, $450.00 for a condemned slave, although the valuations were not made in the form required by law.

1845. Chapter 73. By this act jailors are required to report to court Negroes committed for want of freedom papers; the court shall not permit such Negroes to be hired out longer than two years. The hirer must give bond double the value of the Negro not to remove him from the Commonwealth.

1845. Chapters 149–151. The legal representatives of Mary Stubblefield are allowed $450.00 for a condemned slave when satisfactory evidence is presented that he has been executed; Wm. Nock is allowed $500.00; and Charles T. Grills, $575.00.

1846. Chapter 15. The directors of the Eastern Lunatic Asylum are hereby empowered to receive insane slaves as patients on the application of their owners, if accompanied by security for charges, and provided no slave shall be retained in the asylum to the exclusion of any insane white resident of the state.

1848. Criminal Code. Chapter 120. Section 31. The unlawful importation of a slave born without the United States shall be punishable by a fine of $1,000.00.

1848. Chapter 308. Polly Littlepage Smith is authorized, in her own name, as if she were a feme sole, to file a bill praying the court to permit her to remove certain slaves to Alabama, bond to be given to cause the slaves and their increase to be divided among Polly's children at her death, according to the will bequeathing them.

1848. Chapter 329. Sarah C. Byars is allowed $600.00 for a slave, Jim, condemned by the Smyth County court and reprieved by the executive for sale and transportation.

1849. Chapter 311. The committee having the custody and control of the person and property of Martha Watts, of Campbell County, who is possessed of a large number of slaves but no land on which to maintain them, is authorized on a proper application to the court to sell the said slaves.

1850. Chapter 316. A slave of Mary B. Nelson, condemned to death, was assessed at $425.00 by the court; the governor has commuted the punishment of death to sale and transportation, and it is shown that the court erred in fixing a price for the slave far below his market value. It is therefore enacted that the governor cause to be paid to Mary B. Nelson, the owner of the slave, such sum of money as he may receive upon the sale.

1851. Chapter 51. This act to facilitate the recovery of fugitive slaves requires courts to convene and enter on the records proof of an escape, and a general description of the slave, pursuant to the act of Congress of September 18, 1850, concerning persons escaping.

1851. Chapter 289. The sum of $550.00 is allowed for a slave of F. P. Redman, convicted and ordered transported.

1851. Resolution No. 22. A Negro slave, William, a felon, convicted in Fauquier and his punishment commuted to transportation has since become lunatic and unsaleable, is ordered to be removed from the penitentiary to the Eastern Lunatic Asylum for reasons of humanity as well as other considerations.

1856. Chapter 47. An act intended to provide additional protection for the slave property of citizens of the Commonwealth is passed whereby all vessels owned in whole or in part by any citizen or resident of another state, and about to sail or steam to any port north of and beyond the capes of Virginia (except those bound direct to any foreign counties), shall be inspected. The vessel shall be attached and all persons on board arrested if any slave or person held to service is found on board. Persons apprehending slaves escaping on a vessel trading to or belonging to a non-slaveholding state shall be entitled to a reward of $100.00.

1856. Chapter 48. Any free person, who shall cause to be carried away, or be concerned in the escape of any slave, shall be confined in the penitentiary five to ten years; and, moreover, in lieu of damages forfeit to the owner double the value of the slave, pay reasonable expenses incurred in the attempt to regain the slave, and in the discretion of the jury be publicly whipped to such an extent and at such times

as it may deem fit. No whipping shall exceed thirty-nine
lashes for anybody in any one day. If the offender be in
command or attached to a vessel, it shall be forfeited to the
state. The section includes any master of a vessel, and any free
person traveling by land.

Any master of a vessel who knowingly receives on board a
runaway slave shall be confined in the penitentiary five to ten
years, and forfeit the full value of the slave, be whipped, etc.
If the slave is found on board after leaving port, or in the
night time the person in charge shall be presumed to have
knowingly received him, and if any free white person advise
any slave to abscond, or furnish him money, clothes, provisions, or other facility, he shall be confined five to ten years
in the penitentiary, and be whipped as the jury sees fit. A
slave so persuading or conniving shall be punished with
stripes and sold out of the state. Any free white person who
gives information leading to the conviction of a free white
person engaged in carrying off a slave, or in any manner concerned in helping an escape, shall be entitled to a reward of
$500.00, to be paid by the state.

1856. Chapter 49. This act amends previous legislation
by increasing the reward for the arrest of runaway slaves. In
the case of slaves arrested in a non-slaveholding state and delivered to the owner or a jailer in this Commonwealth, a reward of 25 per cent of the value of the fugitive shall be paid.
If the arrest be in a non-slaveholding state and the person is
entitled to $100.00 or more from the owner, it shall be the
duty of the auditor of public accounts to issue his warrant on
the treasury for $50.00. Rewards and mileage are also allowed
for arrests of runaways in this state.

1856. Chapter 50.   It shall not be lawful for citizens of Virginia to hire a slave or permit a slave to reside in the District of Columbia unless in the service of his owner, and thereafter to permit such slave to return to this state, under a penalty of $50.00, one-half of which is to be paid to the informer.

1858. Chapter 31.   It is enacted that a tenant for life of slaves who removes them out of the state, or sells a greater interest in such slaves than a life estate, is guilty of a felony.

1860. Chapter 2.   No person shall without license buy for sale or sell for others on commission slaves, horses, mules, cattle, sheep or hogs.[11]

1860. Chapter 42.   More effectively to prevent the escape of slaves, the penalty for carrying away a slave is increased to twenty years in the penitentiary.

1861. Chapter 169.   This act authorizes the governor to pardon slaves, Jack and Ben, condemned for sale and transportation and restore them to their former owner, F. N. Fitzhugh.

1861. Chapter 170.   The pardon of a Negro slave, Tom, is authorized.

1861. Chapter 171.   The pardon of a slave, Bill, is authorized.

1861. Chapter 172.   The pardon of John Ricks is authorized.

1862. Chapter 97.   The Auditor of Accounts is ordered to pay out $600.00, $800,00, and $600.00, the assessed value of certain slaves convicted of felony.

---

[11]Many other tax laws contained similar provisions.

1862. Chapter 130. This act authorizes the governor to sell to John Washington, of Caroline County, a slave named Richard, convicted of grand larceny and formerly belonging to the said Washington, provided Washington pay the costs, relinquish all claims against the Commonwealth for his value, and immediately sells the slave beyond the limits of the Commonwealth.

1863. Chapter 82. Sarah T. Thornton, a widow, possessed of a life estate in certain slaves, is authorized to remove them to North Carolina, under bond to deliver them at her death to the persons entitled to them.

1863. Chapter 87. The governor is directed to deliver to B. B. and J. W. Cooley, an infant child of the slave Harriet, who was condemned to be hung, but who died in the jail at Richmond before execution of sentence.

1863. Chapter 88. The sum of $400.00, the appraised value of Harriet, the slave who died, is allowed the owners, B. B. and J. W. Cooley.

1864. Chapter 65. Any person harboring or employing a slave without the master's consent shall forfeit to the master $10.00 to $50.00 for every day of harboring; but this section shall not apply to any person within the lines of the public enemy, unless it shall appear that the same was done with the intent to defraud the owner of the services of the slave, or to deprive the owner of his right of property in such slave.

1864. Chapter 98. Wm. J. Morgan, of Fauquier, is allowed $1,325.00, the value of a slave named Beverly, condemned to be hung, and who committed suicide by hanging prior to his execution.

1866. Chapter 17. This act repeals all acts and parts of acts relating to slaves and slavery.

CHAPTER V

Free Persons of Color and Slaves

1670. Act V. Negroes or Indians, though baptised and enjoying their own freedom, shall be incapable of purchasing Christians, yet they are not deterred from buying any of their own nation.[1]

1691. Act XVI. Negroes who are set free must be transported out of the country by the person giving them freedom within six months after such setting free.[2]

1705. Chapter XLIX. No Negro, although Christian, shall purchase any Christian servant, except of his own complexion, or such as are declared slaves. If any Negro shall purchase any Christian white servant, the servant shall become free.[3]

1723. Chapter IV. No Negro or Indian slave shall be set free upon any pretense whatsoever, except for some meritorious service to be adjudged by the governor.

1780. Chapter XXV. Ned and Kate, slaves, are declared free and may enjoy the rights of free Negroes.

1782. Chapter XXI. It is lawful for any person by last will or other instrument in writing, sealed and witnessed, to emancipate his slaves.

---

[1] Actually there were free Negroes long before this time, although the first legislative reference to them seems to have been in 1668. See Chapter VI; also Chapter II.
[2] See Chapter II for fuller statement of this law.
[3] See Chapter III for fuller statement.

Liberated slaves neglecting to pay tax levies may be hired out by the sheriff long enough to raise the taxes.[4]

1788. Chapter XXXVII. Whoever steals a free person, knowing him to be free, shall suffer death.

1793. Chapter 22. Free Negroes or mulattoes shall be registered and numbered in a book to be kept by the town clerk, which shall specify age, name, color, status and by whom, and in what court emancipated. Annually the Negro shall be delivered a copy for twenty-five cents. A penalty is fixed for employing a Negro without a certificate; the Negro may be committed to jail. Every free Negro shall once in every three years obtain a new certificate.

1793. Chapter 23. This act forbids free Negroes or mulattoes from migrating into the Commonwealth. If they come in, they may be exported to the place from which they came.

Every master of a vessel or other person who shall bring into this Commonwealth by water or by land any free Negro shall forfeit one hundred pounds, one-half to the Commonwealth and the other half to the informer.

1801. Chapter 70. It is the duty of commissioners of the revenue annually to return a complete list of all free Negroes within their districts, with their names, sex, place of abode, and trades; a copy of the list shall be fixed at the courthouse door.

If any free Negro so registered shall remove into another county it shall be lawful for the magistrate of the place where he may intrude to issue a warrant to apprehend the free

---

[4]Until the time of the Civil War free Negroes could be hired out to pay their taxes but at that time not for taxes in arrears more than five years.

Negro; if it be proved he has no honest employment, he shall be treated as a vagrant.

1803. Chapter 23. Robt. Brown, formerly of Richmond, did in his lifetime emancipate two slaves, afterward known as Billy Brown and Sally Brown, and did also by his will devise them certain real and personal estate. Billy Brown having died intestate and unmarried, the Commonwealth herewith relinquishes its rights in favor of Sally Brown.[5]

1806. Chapter 94. A free Negro is not to carry any fire-lock of any kind without a license. For a second offense he shall in addition to forfeiting all such arms be punished with stripes, at the discretion of the justice not exceeding thirty-nine.

1810. Chapter LVIII. A certain free man of color, by the name of Frank, has died, leaving in bondage a widow, Patience, and three children, whom Frank, by meritorious industry, purchased in his lifetime, but failed to emancipate; it is enacted by the General Assembly that Patience and the children shall be free.

1810. Chapter LXXVIII. Pompey Branch, a free black man, is permitted to remain as a free person of color in the state.

1811. Chapter XXX. Whereas it has been represented that watermen navigating James River and its branches above the falls at Richmond commit depredations on the property of the inhabitants bordering on each side, it is enacted that there be appointed an inspector of boats and no free Negro shall be allowed to carry on board his boat any gun or other fire-

---

[5]For earlier acts conferring freedom on slaves see Chapter II and Chapter III, ante.

arms under pain of forfeiting the same to any white person who may seize them; nor shall any owner of a slave permit him to carry such arms.

Any waterman of color found strolling from his boat may be whipped with any number of lashes, not exceeding twenty, if he is not going directly to or from any spring for the purpose of getting water.[6]

1811. Chapter XLIX. A penalty of $20.00 is set for free Negroes who cut down or destroy trees, or commit waste in the undergrowth at Old Point Comfort. Slaves shall receive thirty-nine lashes on their bare backs, well laid on. Owners of vessels may be arrested and their boats detained until penalties are paid.

1811. Chapters LXXIX–LXXX. Jingo and James Lott, free men of color, are permitted to remain in the state. Hannah, liberated by William Turner, may also remain.

1811. Chapter LXXXIV. It is enacted that additional powers be given the trustees of Portsmouth to prevent the practice of galloping horses and mules in the streets, to prohibit hogs running at large, and to restrain Negroes from wandering about the streets at night, or on Sundays or other holidays.

1812. Chapter CXXVIII. A slave, Jacob, is permitted to be emancipated in pursuance of a will but is not to remain in this state.

1812. Chapter CXXIX. Fincastle Sterrit, formerly the property of Wm. King, who emancipated him, is permitted to remain in the state.

---

[6]The act provides penalties for watermen being free, or owners of slaves for stealing or burning rails, or wood, stealing grain, etc.

1812. Chapter CXXX. Sam, the property of Edward Digges, after emancipation may remain in this state and enjoy the privileges of a free person of color.

1812. Chapters CXXXI–CXXXV. These five acts permit various persons of color to remain in the state after emancipation.

1813. Chapters CXXXI–CXXXII. Ben Johnston, a free man of color, is permitted to reside in this state; also Franky, a free woman of color, formerly the property of Chas. Beckley, is permitted to remain.

1814. Chapter CV. In January, James, a resident of Hampshire County, a free man of color, is permitted to remain in the Commonwealth.

In December, a Negro woman named Hynah is permitted to remain in the Commonwealth as a free person.[7]

1814. Chapter CVI. In January, James, a man of color, who had been promised his freedom if he paid $600.00 to his master, which condition has now been complied with, when emancipated, may remain in the Commonwealth as a free person.

In December, Armistead, sometimes called Armistead Smith, a man of exemplary character, had an equitable right to freedom previous to the passage of the law prohibiting emancipated persons of color from remaining in this state; he is permitted to remain.[7]

1814. Chapters CVII- CVIII. In January and December of this year, Ben, otherwise called Benjamin Godwin, is per-

---

[7] The acts are different, the numbers and years the same.

mitted to remain as a free person of color; also Daniel, Jacob and Mary; also Sterling, who had been left money by his mistress to purchase his freedom before the passage of the act; and many others.

1814. Chapter CIX. This act permits George Butler, who is an old man, to remain because he is attached to his family, who are slaves, and cannot be taken from the state.

1816. Resolution No. 1. The General Assembly of Virginia has sought to obtain an asylum beyond the United States for free persons of color, but has been frustrated: They now avail themselves of a period when peace has healed the wounds of humanity, and the principal nations of Europe have concurred with the government of the United States in abolishing the African slave trade (a traffic which this Commonwealth, both before and since the Revolution, zealously sought to exterminate), to renew this effort; and resolve that the executive of Virginia correspond with the President of the United States for the purpose of obtaining a territory upon the coast of Africa, or the shore of the North Pacific, not within the United States, to serve as an asylum for free persons of color.[8]

1818. Chapter CXCVII. A judgment on a bond given by two people for Hoomes, a free man of color convicted of a felony, is released because they, by their exertions, afterward brought the said Hoomes to justice.

---

[8]The hope of colonizing Negroes outside the country has not died in Virginia. By joint resolution the Assembly in February, 1936, memorialized "the Congress of the United States to make provision for the colonization of persons of African descent with their consent in Liberia or at any other place or places on the African continent." This resolution passed both houses but is not printed in the 1936 session laws as the custom of including resolutions with the printed laws no longer prevails in the state.

1819. Chapter CLXXXVIII. A certain Izard Bacon, of the county of Henrico, by will did set free all his slaves, and the dictates of justice and humanity require the right of freedom of the said slaves should be confirmed; the Chancellor of the Superior Court of Chancery of Richmond is authorized to give the slaves their freedom, taking care that none remain within the Commonwealth more than twelve months.

1820. Chapter XXVI. Overseers of the poor once every three months are to examine into the condition of all free Negroes and mulattoes, and unless it shall appear that by their own labor they procure sufficient means for substinance, they shall be deemed vagrants. They shall also be deemed vagrants if they trade with slaves without the leave of their masters.

1820. Chapter CXXXIII. Chas. Cousins, a free man of color, about eighteen years previously had married Aggy, who in a short time was sold to Thomas Howlett, who purchased Aggy for Charles. Charles Cousins repaid Howlett the purchase price of his wife. Cousins has children by a former marriage, who under existing laws would become the owners of his wife if he were to die suddenly. The Assembly declares that when Aggy is regularly emancipated by Cousins she may remain in the Commonwealth as a free person.

1822. Chapter 111. Swan Hambleton and his wife, Sarah, persons of color, who were emancipated by their master, John Skidmore, for general good conduct and for defending two of his children against the savage fury of the Indians, in the early settlement of Lee County, have had great difficulty in obtaining a court composed of a majority of the acting magistrates of Lee County, as required; it is therefore enacted that the said Swan Hambleton and his wife may reside in the Commonwealth for twelve months or until they have a court hearing, although a majority of the justices are not present.

1822. Chapter 112. Reuben Howard, of Hanover, by will emancipated all of his slaves and did devise them his land and other property, and directed his executor to take such course with the Negroes as he might think proper; the executor has petitioned the legislature to authorize him to sell the land and remove the Negroes from the Commonwealth. It is enacted that the emancipated persons by court proceedings may be decreed free and the court shall have the power to sell the land and direct the money arising therefrom to be appropriated for the use of the emancipated persons and to pay their removal expenses out of the Commonwealth.

1823. Chapter 32. Henceforth, when any free Negro shall be convicted of an offense, now by law punished by imprisonment for more than two years, such person instead of confinement shall be punished by stripes at the discretion of the jury, and shall moreover be adjudged to be sold as a slave and banished beyond the limits of the United States.

1823. Chapter 33. If a slave or free Negro shall wilfully assault and beat a white person with an intention to kill, on conviction he shall be punished by stripes at the discretion of the jury or court and, moreover, be banished from the United States forever. If such convict at any time shall return, he shall suffer death without benefit of clergy.

1824. Chapter 101. Dennis Holley, a free man of color, being sick and unable to leave the state within the time limit, is now permitted to remain a year.

1825. Chapter 102. Robert Trout, a free man of color, lately emancipated, is permitted to remain in the Commonwealth one year to enable him to sell his property and collect his debts before departure.

1825. Chapter 103. A slave, Jack, otherwise called John Booker, paid his master $700.00 for his freedom, but afterward the law of 1806 prohibited slaves from remaining in the Commonwealth, so he was conveyed to one Henry Hoxall, of Petersburg, owner of the wife of the said Jack. The said slave has acquired considerable property, and is permitted to remain in Petersburg. If he should be found guilty of any offense, he shall be ordered to leave.

1825. Chapter 104. Lewis Bowlah, a man of color, now in Richmond, who was previously for an act of extraordinary merit emancipated in Louisiana, is permitted to remain, subject to revocation if guilty of an offense.

1825. Chapter 105. Jerry, otherwise called Jerry Peebles, is permitted to remain in the counties of Greenbrier and Nicholas, with some exception.

1826. Chapter 61. No person other than a free white citizen of the Commonwealth shall be allowed to pilot a vessel up or down the Rappahannock River.

1826. Chapter 137. Jacob Spengler, a free man of color, is permitted to remain in Rockingham County, subject to revocation if guilty of an offense.

1827. Chapter 26. Overseers of the poor are not hereafter to sell Negroes or mulattoes emancipated since 1806 who remain in the state more than twelve months.

Grand juries shall inquire into the cases of Negroes or mulattoes remaining without leave more than twelve months after emancipation, and proceedings shall be had as in the cases of misdemeanor; after verdict by jury or confession of party, he or she shall be sold by the sheriff or sergeant. The money arising from the sale shall be paid into the treasury for the Literary Fund.

1827. Chapter 139. Burwell, Joe Fossett, John Hemmings, Madison and Eston Hemmings, persons of color, emancipated by the will of Thos. Jefferson, deceased, are permitted to remain as free persons within this Commonwealth, provided they are not hereafter convicted by the verdict of a jury and the judgment of the court of an offense against the Commonwealth.

1828. Chapter 37. Free persons of color, who are hereafter convicted of any offense, the punishment of which is stripes, transportation and sale, shall for the first offense be confined in jail or penitentiary for from five to eighteen years; punishment for succeeding offenses, life.

1828. Chapter 153. One Wm. Ashby, Sheriff of Culpeper, is allowed such a sum as may be just for the support and clothes for certain Negroes who were allowed their freedom in another case, taking into consideration the value of their labor to Ashby.

1828. Chapter 163. Fifty dollars is allowed the jailor of Nelson County for keeping a Negro supposed to be a runaway in jail, from September 16, 1826, to November 28, 1827, when he was set at liberty by the court under a belief that he was a free man.

1828. Chapter 167. Ben Hord, a man of color, emancipated by will, is permitted to remain in the Commonwealth, but a majority of the court may revoke the leave of residence when they shall think fit; if revoked and he remains, he shall forfeit his freedom.

1828. Chapter 168. David Ward, a man of color, emancipated by will, is permitted to remain, but if convicted of an offense, the leave to remain may be revoked.

1828. Chapter 169. Lydia, a free woman of color, of Greenbrier, is permitted to remain in the Commonwealth in consideration of uniform good conduct for one year after the death of the owner of her father and mother, who will then be free also. If she remains longer, she shall forfeit her freedom and be subject to sale. The court may at any time require Lydia to give security for her good behavior; moreover, she shall remove from the Commonwealth all children she may have living.

1828. Chapter 170. Ten slaves, owned by the late Jane Barr, and by her given their freedom by will, are permitted to remain for five years, but no longer in the Commonwealth; security for their good conduct may be required, and if they do not depart they shall forfeit their freedom; no descendant of these persons is to remain beyond the period set.

1828. Chapter 179. Certain free persons of color are permitted to remain for five years, one of them having contracted to buy her husband for $620.00, which sum she expects to pay within five years.

1828. Chapter 180. Michael Smith, a free man of color, is permitted to remain for a limited time to finish paying for his wife. If he remains longer than the date set, he shall forfeit his freedom.

1829. Chapter 177. The punishment of Philip Brumskill, a man of color, condemned to slavery, transportation and sale is commuted to confinement in the penitentiary for six years, in solitary confinement on low and coarse diet for one-twentieth of the time.

1829. Chapter 178. This act permits Elizabeth Boswell, of Rockingham County, who is fifty years of age, to remain in the Commonwealth, subject to revocation if she is convicted of crime. Elizabeth was purchased by her husband and emancipated; he is now too old to sustain the difficulties of removing to another country and they have acquired sufficient property to support them in comfort where they are.

1829. Chapter 181. Richard Greenway, a man of color and good character, emancipated by the will of Isaac Parham, of Prince George County, is permitted to remain in the county, but the county court shall have the power to revoke the leave whenever they deem it expedient; if he remain more than twelve months after revocation, he shall forfeit his freedom and be subject to sale.

1830. Chapter 129. The executor of James Bray, deceased, of Chesterfield County, is authorized to sell several tracts of land, and a mill left to twenty-five slaves emancipated by the will, and invest the money in land, lying out of Virginia and in the state in which the emancipated slaves shall determine to remove or shall have removed.

1830. Chapter 150. Dilly, a free woman of color, emancipated in 1827 by recorded deed, received no certificate, so that after twelve months her right to freedom was forfeited. The owner of her husband is willing for her to reside with him. She is hereby restored to freedom and permitted to remain in the county of Giles for one year and no longer, unless in the meantime the county court of Giles shall give her permission to remain.

1830. Chapter 151. Wm. Strother, a man of color, recently emancipated, has a slave wife upwards of sixty years of age, and is permitted to remain in the Commonwealth provided not convicted of an offense.

1831. Chapter XXXIX. Free Negroes and mulattoes who remain in the Commonwealth contrary to law are to be sold publicly.

1831. Chapter CCXXXI. The Commonwealth's right to the personal estate of Moses Cross, deceased, a free man of color, late of Goochland County, by reason of failure of relatives of said Moses, is released to Jacob Sampson, a free man of color, and Frankey, his wife, the natural child of the said Moses, provided that Jacob Sampson shall emancipate Frankey and all her children.

1832. Chapter XXII. Amending an act entitled "an act reducing into one the several acts concerning slaves, free Negroes, and mulattoes and for other purposes," it is enacted that no slave, free Negro or mulatto shall preach, or hold any meeting for religious purposes either day or night; any slave or free Negro so offending shall be punished at the discretion of the justice of the peace with not exceeding thirty-nine lashes. Slaves and free Negroes who attend any religious meeting conducted by any slave or free Negro preacher, ordained or otherwise, and slaves who attend any preaching at night, although conducted by a white minister, without the permission of the master, shall also be punished by stripes and may for that purpose be apprehended by any person without any written or other precept. Masters may, however, permit their slaves, employed or bound, and free Negroes to go with them to religious worship conducted by a white minister. Also religious instruction may be given in the day time by a licensed white minister to slaves and free Negroes.

The slaves of any one master may assemble together for religious devotion.

No free Negro shall hereafter be capable of acquiring ownership, except by descent, to any slave other than his or her husband, wife or children.

Free Negroes are not to carry firelocks of any kind, under penalty of thirty-nine lashes. Permission heretofore granted authorizing justices to permit slaves and free Negroes to carry firearms in some cases is repealed.

Slaves and free Negroes are not permitted to sell or give away ardent or spiritous liquor near any public assembly, under penalty of thirty-nine lashes.

If a slave or free Negro write or print anything advising persons of color to commit insurrection or rebellion, he is to be punished by thirty-nine lashes; if the person offending be white, he is to be fined from $10.00 to $100.00.

Riots and unlawful assembly, trespasses and seditious speeches by free Negroes shall hereafter be punished with stripes, as directed for slaves.

Simple larceny by free Negroes is to be tried and punished as heretofore directed for slaves.[9]

If any white person or free Negro shall knowingly receive from any slave or free Negro any stolen goods, he shall be punished in the same manner as if he had actually stolen the goods.

Free Negroes hereafter shall be tried and punished for felony in the same manner as slaves are now tried, except in cases of homicide and where the punishment is death.

1832. Chapter CCXLVIII. Abraham Depp, a man of color, emancipated by will, is allowed to reside in Powhatan County two years and no longer. This privilege is granted to enable him to dispose of property devised him by his late master.

1833. Chapter 12. The sum of $18,000 is hereby appropriated annually for a period of five years for the transporting and subsistence of free persons of color to or in Liberia or other places on the western coast of Africa by the American Colonization Society. Not more than $30.00 shall be allowed for such persons above the age of ten years, not more than $20.00 for those under ten years.[10]

1833. Chapter 80. County courts are authorized to grant a certificate to any free white person of mixed blood, not being a white person, nor a free Negro, that he or she is

[9]See page 163, Chapter VII.
[10]See page 139, Chapter VI.

not a free Negro, which certificate shall be sufficient to protect such person against the disabilities imposed by law on free Negroes.

1833. Chapter 244. Certain free persons of color, emancipated by Abraham Van Meter, late of the county of Hardy, are permitted to remain in this Commonwealth until the death of the widow of the said Van Meter and one year afterward and no longer, to permit them to dispose of their property devised to them by their master and to make such other arrangements as may be necessary. The permit may be revoked if any of the persons of color are convicted by a jury of an offense.

1833. Chapter 245. One Moses Herdman, a free man of color, of Rockingham County, is permitted to remain two years in the county to reduce a legacy to possession.

1834. Chapter 3. No person having obtained a license shall be permitted to authorize any Negro, bond or free, to exhibit any public show, or to vend any goods as a barker or a peddler.

1834. Chapter 68. A free Negro shall not migrate into this Commonwealth from any state in this Union, or from any foreign country, under penalty of thirty-nine lashes on his bare back at the public whipping post. Returning after removal is to be punished according to the act of 1819. Special fines and penalties are set for masters of vessels who bring in any free Negroes. An exception is made for travelers who have any free Negroes in their employment.

If any free person shall advise or persuade any slave to abscond, or shall furnish any slave any pass, or any money, clothes, or provisions to aid such slave to abscond, every such person, being free, shall be guilty of felony and shall be imprisoned for from two to five years. If a slave shall commit, or aid such offense, he shall receive thirty-nine lashes; on a second conviction he shall be deemed a felon, within the benefit of clergy, and on a third conviction he shall receive thirty-nine lashes and be banished.

It shall not be lawful for the court clerk to register any free Negro unless on court order. In addition to the particulars now required, such register shall specify marks or scars, and by what instrument, deed or will such Negro was emancipated and so on.

1834. Chapter 269. Randal Evans, a man of color, is permitted to remain five years in order to purchase his wife and children.

1834. Chapter 270. Archy Higginbotham, a free man of color, is permitted to remain, subject to the power of the court to revoke the leave.

1834. Chapter 271. Dolly Woodson, a free woman of color, is permitted to remain in Richmond, unless convicted of an offense.

1834. Chapter 272. William Caswell, of Richmond, whose wife and children are entitled to a residence in the Commonwealth, having been born free, is permitted to remain, subject to the usual limitation.

1834. Chapter 273. Jacob and Sealy Woods, free persons of color, advanced in years, and Jacob while a slave, having performed sundry meritorious acts tending to promote the public safety, are permitted to remain in Scott County, subject to revocation.

1834. Chapter 274. Samuel and Celia Leonard are permitted to remain in Halifax County, subject to revocation, they being childless and above sixty years of age and having been devised property by the will of their late mistress.

1835. Chapters 213–227. These are special acts permitting persons of color who have been emancipated, or who have purchased their freedom, to remain in the Commonwealth for limited or unlimited periods, for various reasons.

1836. Chapter 73. In this act to regulate the conduct of certain boatmen it is enacted that when any free Negro shall give a manifest of any loading put on board a boat, he shall obtain a certificate from some respectable white person certifying the truth of the manifest.

1836. Chapters 273–274. Richard Bolling, a free man of color, of Cabell County, is permitted to remain in the state, unless convicted of crime; Daniel Higginbotham is permitted to remain four years to acquire the means of removing himself and family.

1836. Chapters 275–283. These also permit free persons of color to remain, most of them for a limited time.

1837. Chapter 70. Whereas, many petitions are annually presented to the legislature from emancipated slaves praying to remain in the Commonwealth, it is enacted that any slave emancipated since May 1, 1806, may apply to the court for permission to remain. On satisfactory proof that the person is of good character, peaceable, orderly and industrious, and not addicted to drunkeness, gaming or other vice, after notice at the court house door for two months, three-fourths of the justices present concurring, permission to remain within the Commonwealth may be granted during the good pleasure of the court. Accomac and Northampton Counties are exempt from the provisions of this act.

1838. Chapter 99. If free Negroes, whether infant or adult, go beyond the limits of the Commonwealth to be educated, it shall not be lawful for them to return; if infants they shall be bound out as apprentices until twenty-one years, and then sent out of the state; if adults they shall be sent out of the Commonwealth.

1839. Chapter 31. Patrols are authorized to force open the doors of free Negroes and of slaves in the absence of their masters, when access is denied, when in search of firearms or other weapons, by authority of a warrant.

1839. Chapter 84. Hereafter when any free person of color shall be bound out by court order as an apprentice, the court shall consider what the reasonable value of his services shall be for each year of the apprenticeship; if the apprentice shall have a father or mother, the master shall pay him or her the value of his services. If there be no father or mother, then the same shall be paid to the overseers of the poor, and in either case the last year's service shall be paid the apprentice. Nothing in the act shall be construed to take away from the common council of the city of Richmond the authority over the poor of the said corporation.

1839. Chapter 277. The Commonwealth's right to Emma, a woman of color, the property of her husband, who died intestate leaving no heirs, is relinquished and she is permitted to remain in the county of Washington.

1839. Chapter 278. This act permits two free women of color, about sixty years of age, to remain in the Commonwealth provided they give bond payable to the overseers of the poor, conditioned on good behaviour, and not to become chargeable to the county of the Isle of Wight.

1840. Chapter 200. It is enacted by the General Assembly that it shall be lawful for the court of Giles County to license Thomas Beasley, a free man of color, to carry a firelock and also powder and lead.

1841. Chapter 74. If any person secrete or aid in secreting any slave or free Negro, or send any slave or free Negro out of the county where he has committed an offense, he shall be punished by a penalty for the use of the overseers of the poor. The act authorizing free Negroes to be carried out of the state at public expense is repealed. After August next, free Negroes are prohibited from coming into the state, except as servants of white persons, who do not remain more than five days.

A fee of $1.00 shall be paid to the person or officer apprehending, and the free Negro shall give bond to quit the state. On failure to give bond, the prisoner shall be sentenced to not more than thirty-nine lashes, which punishment may be repeated once in every week so long as the free Negro remains in the Commonwealth.

1842. Chapter 225. Charles Bruce and nine of his relatives, free persons of color, are permitted to remain four years to dispose of their estate devised to them by their late mistress, Elizabeth Van Meter.

1843. Chapter 86. Free Negroes in Accomac and Richmond counties are not to sell or barter corn, wheat, peas or other agricultural products without a certificate in writing of two respectable white persons of the neighborhood stating that the Negro raised the same or came honestly by it. Any Negroes offending shall forfeit the products. The proceeds, after compensation has been paid to the officer, shall go to the overseers of the poor, and the Negro shall moreover be punished by not exceeding fifteen lashes. White persons wilfully purchasing products from a free Negro without a certificate shall be guilty of a misdemeanor.

1843. Chapter 87. If any slave or free Negro shall sell, prepare or administer, except under the direction of his master, any medicine of any kind, he shall be guilty of a misdemeanor and shall be punished with stripes, not exceeding thirty-nine, on his bare back. If any free Negro shall cause to be administered any drug or substance causing abortion, he shall be confined five to ten years; if a slave, he shall receive thirty-nine lashes, and for a second offense, suffer death without benefit of clergy.

1844. Chapter 152. The legislature declares George and Henry Angus, persons of color of Petersburg, free; the will of their mother, a free person of color, emancipating them not being properly attested.

1846. Chapter 93. If any free Negro shall hereafter commit simple larceny of any thing to the value of $20.00 or less, he may be tried by any justice of the peace of the county or city in which the crime was committed, and upon conviction, instead of the punishment now prescribed, he shall be punished by not exceeding thirty-nine lashes; if acquitted, the acquittal shall be final.

1846. Chapter 94. The punishment of free Negroes who assault and beat white persons with intent to kill is made confinement of five to eighteen years.

1846. Chapter 95. Whenever a colored person is charged with any crime, as a free person, any person who claims such person of color may assert his claim and a jury must determine the claim.

If any person of color shall be confined in the jail or penitentiary under sentence as a free person, the question whether the person is or is not the slave of a petitioner shall be tried by a jury; the Commonwealth's Attorney shall act as counsel for the prisoner, as well as for the Commonwealth. If the person is found to be a slave, he shall be delivered to the owner, who shall give bond conditioned to have the slave delivered for prosecution, unless he is fairly sold at public auction and removed from Virginia.

1847. Chapter 235. The interest of the state to the estate of Thomas Walden, of "Blandford," Petersburg, a free carpenter of color, is released to Nancy Munford, alias Walden, Elizabeth Armistead, late Elizabeth Walden, and Catherine Walden, who claim to be the rightful and natural heirs of Thomas Walden.

1847. Chapter 286. The sentence of Jane Hailstock, a free woman of color, found guilty of arson, is ordered commuted.

1847. Chapters 287–89. James L. Campbell, Julia Ann Wilson, Thomas Duncan, George Scott, and Lucy Scott, persons of color, are permitted to remain in the Commonwealth.

1848. Resolution No. 5. This resolution instructs the directors of lunatic asylums to report to the next Assembly upon the propriety and cost of providing for the maintenance and care of insane persons of color; in case they deem it inexpedient to provide for such patients in their respective hospitals, to report a plan for the separate accommodation of such patients.

1848. Chapter 108. The act requiring the hire of colored apprentices which have neither father or mother to be paid to overseers of the poor is hereby repealed. Money received by an overseer is to be paid to the apprentice at the expiration of his term of apprenticeship.

Hereafter also a bond shall be taken from the master to cover the reasonable annual value of the services of the apprentice. If there are parents, they are to receive the value of the apprentice's service, except the last year's service, or when the court may for good cause order all the payment to be held for the benefit of the apprentice.

1848. Criminal Code. Chapter 120. The rape or abuse of a female child above ten years of age or under, with her consent, by a white person, is punishable by penitentiary sentence of from ten to twenty years; if by a free Negro death, or at discretion of the jury confinement of from five to twenty years.

Any free person who sells a free person as a slave shall be confined in the penitentiary from three to ten years.

Any person emancipated from slavery since May 1, 1806, or claiming his right to freedom under an ancestor emancipated since that day, who shall remain in the state more than one year after his freedom accrued, and more than one year after he arrives at the age of twenty-one, or more than one year after the revocation of any lawful permission to remain shall forfeit his right to freedom and be sold as a slave.

Any free person who shall bring into this state any free Negro shall be confined in jail not more than six months and fined not exceeding $500.00, with an exception for those traveling into or through the state with a free Negro as a servant.

It shall not be lawful for any free Negro to come into this state; one coming in shall be apprehended, and give bond conditioned to depart within ten days and not return. In default of giving such a bond the free Negro shall be punished by stripes not exceeding thirty-nine, which punishment may be repeated from time to time, so long as the free Negro shall remain in this state. The law does not extend to a free Negro in the employment of a person traveling into or through the state, if not sojourning longer than thirty days.

Any free person of color who shall migrate from the state, or who shall for the purpose of being educated be sent from the state, or who shall for any purpose go to a non-slaveholding state, shall be no longer entitled to residence in Virginia, and on returning may be proceeded against as directed.[11]

1849. Chapter 353–358.   These sections authorize certain free persons of color to remain in the state by court action, with the usual stipulations.

[11] In 1860 there were still prohibitions against free Negroes remaining in the state without lawful permission, migrating into the state, penalties for white persons bringing free Negroes in, free Negroes going out for education, etc.

1850. Chapter 17. This act provides certain money for additional accommodations for free colored persons at the Eastern Lunatic Asylum.

1850. Chapter 338. The Hustings Court of Richmond is authorized to grant permission to Arthur, a free man of color, to remain in the Commonwealth during the pleasure of the court.

1850. Chapter 339. Susan Blackwell, a free person of color, of Norfolk, by accompanying Dr. Henry W. Tabb to Massachusetts last summer as a servant incurred certain penalties, but she is restored hereby to her rights as a free woman of color, and discharged from all pains and forfeitures.

1850. Chapters 340–345. Free persons of color are permitted to remain if the courts agree.

1851. Chapter 66. Not more than two dogs shall be allowed on farms in Middlesex, except they be hounds, and in that case five may remain on the premises, provided that no slave or free Negro shall, unless a license be obtained, under any pretense keep a dog of any description, nor shall a slave or free Negro be permitted to pass through Middlesex County having a dog with him, without permission in writing from the owner of the slave or dog; punishments for violations are not to exceed thirty-nine lashes.

1852. Chapter 365. An act revising and reducing into one act the provisions of the charter of the City of Richmond says in section thirty that the city council may prevent hogs, dogs, and other animals from running at large; they may prohibit Negroes from raising hogs or keeping dogs; and they may prevent the riding or driving of horses or other animals, or the running of steam engines at an improper speed. Section thirty-two provides that the owners or employers of Negroes in the city may be required to provide them with board and lodging, under penalties. The council may declare what constitutes an unlawful assemblage of Negroes in the city.

1853. Chapter 55. The sum of $30,000 is appropriated for five years for the removal of free Negroes from the Commonwealth. The Colonization Board of Virginia is given power to act under this law. The annual tax of one dollar is levied on every male free Negro of twenty-one years and under fifty-five years, and collected as other taxes on free Negroes are collected. The fund arising from this source shall be applied to the removal of free Negroes.[12]

1854. Chapter 207. This act provides for the voluntary enslavement of Willis and Andrew, free persons of color in the County of Lunenberg, who were emancipated by the last will of David Doswell. Should the said free persons of color select masters among the next of kin of the said Doswell, it shall be lawful for them to file petitions setting forth their desire, and if the court is satisfied that there is no fraud or collusion between the parties and that the petitioners will be the bona fide slaves of the person designated, the fee simple property in said Negroes as slaves shall rest in the person chosen as master.

1856. Chapter 46. It shall be lawful for any free person of color, of the age of eighteen if a female, and twenty-one if a

---

[12]Acts of 1849 and 1850 replaced by this.

male, to choose a master by court petition. The value of the Negro shall be ascertained and the individual chosen as master shall pay into court one-half of such valuation, and enter into bond, in such penalty as the court may prescribe, with condition that the said Negro shall not become chargeable to any county or city. The property in said Negro as a slave shall vest in the person chosen as master, and the condition of the petitioner shall in all respects be the same as though the Negro had been born a slave, but the children of any such female free person of color previously born shall not be reduced to slavery.

1856. Chapter 51.   It shall not be lawful for any druggists to sell any free Negro or any slave any poisonous drug, without the written permission of the owner or master.

1856. Chapters 432–435.   These are acts for the voluntary enslavement of Thomas Grayson, a free person of color, of Culpeper; of Simon and Martha, his wife, and Judy and Margaret, his daughters, of Southampton; Lewis Williamson, of Southampton; Araminta Frances and Dangerfield, of Culpeper, by court petitions.

1858. Chapter 29.   The governor shall at his discretion employ upon public works owned by the Commonwealth any free Negro sentenced to the penitentiary, likewise any slave sentenced to sale and transportation.

1858. Chapter 47.   No free Negro shall be capable of acquiring, except by descent, any slave.

1858. Chapters 62–63.   Wine or ardent spirits, or a mixture thereof, shall not be sold to any free Negro, unless upon the written certificate of three or more justices of the peace that the said free Negro is sober and orderly and of good character.

1860. Chapter 2. No license shall be granted to a free Negro to keep an ordinary or otherwise to sell ardent spirits.

No license shall be deemed to authorize any show or exhibitions in any town contrary to the ordinances of the corporation, or to authorize any free Negro to take part in such show.

1860. Chapter 54. If any free Negro commit an offense punishable by confinement in the penitentiary, he may at the discretion of the court, in lieu of such confinement, be sold into absolute slavery.

1860. Chapters 281-282. These acts provide for the voluntary enslavement of Mary, a Negro woman, and her children, emancipated by the will of Nelson Colvin, and Martha Brown, a free Negro, of Giles County, of the age of twenty-three years.

1861. Chapter 26. This act for the voluntary enslavement of free Negroes states that on the enslavement of a mother having children, and if there be no mother, then of the father having children, the master chosen shall be required to take the custody, control and service of such children as are free, until the females arrive at eighteen years and the males at twenty-one, and shall pay for his or her services at the expiration thereof, so much and for such years as the court may order.[13]

---

[13]There were 58,042 free Negroes in Virginia at this time, who could have applied to the court to permit them to choose a master or mistress, but comparatively few availed themselves of the privilege.

1861. Chapter 165. This act provides for the voluntary enslavement of George, Shed, Sam, and Sukey, Negroes manumitted by Archibald T. Gordon.

1861. Chapters 166–168. These sections provide for the voluntary enslavement of six other persons of color.

1863. Chapter 14. This act amends previous acts to suppress gaming and sets a penalty for a free person who keeps or exhibits a gaming table, of confinement in jail of two to twelve months, fine of $100.00 to $1,000.00; and at the discretion of the court stripes on his bare back, not exceeding thirty-nine. Betting or playing at such a table or bank is also punishable. If a free Negro knowingly engages as a servant in a house kept for unlawful gaming, he shall be declared to be a slave for life and be sold into slavery.

1864. Chapter 106. The Auditor of Public Accounts is authorized to return $285.00 to Wm. E. Prince, of Sussex County, the same having been paid by Prince under a misapprehension of the law, for the purchase of a free Negro named Billy Barlow allowed to enslave himself in 1863.

1866. Chapter 15. No contract between a white and a colored person for the labor or service of the latter for a longer period than two months shall be binding on such colored person, unless in writing, signed by the white person and the colored person before a justice, notary, clerk of the court, or overseer of the poor, or two or more credible witnesses. It shall be the duty of the justice, notary, clerk, overseers, or witnesses to read and explain the contract to the colored person.

If any person entice away from the service of another any laborer employed by him under contract, he shall forfeit to the party aggrieved from $10.00 to $20.00.[14]

1866. Chapter 17. This act repeals Chapter One Hundred and Seven of the Virginia Code relating to free Negroes.

1866. Chapter 28. Whereas, there has lately been a great increase of idle and disorderly persons, it is enacted that vagrants may be ordered to be employed for a term not exceeding three months, and to be hired out for the best wages that can be procured. If any vagrant run away, he may be returned to the custody of the hirer, who shall have free of any further hire the services of the vagrant for one month in addition to the original term, and the employer may be authorized to work the vagrant, confined with ball and chain. If the employer refuses to take the vagrant back, he may be employed on public works, confined with ball and chain, or in the jail on bread and water.

Vagrants are defined to be, those who return to any county after being lawfully removed, those who live idly and refuse to work for the usual wages, those who refuse to perform the work allotted by the overseer of the poor, beggars (unless incapable of labor), those from without the Commonwealth who have no visible means of subsistence.

1866. Chapter 142. Whereas, the recent radical change in the labor system of the South has rendered the introduction of a new class of laborers necessary; therefore, to encourage and protect the importation of persons for this purpose, it is enacted that contracts for a term of service not exceeding two

---

[14]Chap. 89, 1871. This act repeals Chapter 15 of 1865-66 in regard to contracts of labor between white and colored persons.

years, made in a foreign country, shall be respected and enforced by this state.

1867. Chapter 238. The act to regulate contracts for labor between white and colored persons and to impose a fine on a person enticing laborers from the service of their employers is amended, making the person guilty of the misdemeanor of enticing laborers away punishable by a fine of $20.00 to $100.00, and he may be required to enter into a recognizance for good behavior and in addition forfeit to the party aggrieved $10.00 to $20.00 for every such offense.

1870. Chapter 146. This act provides for the establishment of a lunatic asylum to be known as the Central Lunatic Asylum for the reception and treatment of colored persons of unsound mind, to be located temporarily at Howard's Grove, near the City of Richmond.

1882. Chapter 245. The directors of the Central Lunatic Asylum are authorized to erect suitable buildings for the colored insane at Petersburg, on land donated by the City of Petersburg.[15]

---

[15]The Central State Hospital is still the only institution for Negro insane and feeble-minded in Virginia.

CHAPTER VI

Taxes, Civil Rights and Duties of Negroes and Others

1623. For defraying public debts our troubles have brought upon us, there shall be levied ten pounds of tobacco upon every male head above sixteen years.

1629. Act V. No person working the ground, which are all to be tithable, should plant above 3,000 tobacco plants upon an head, with an exception where the family consists only of children and women which do not work in the ground, and they do not plant above 1,000 plants per poll.[1]

1629. Act VI. To defray the charges for powder, shot, wine, fish, and maintaining three Indians here residing, the Assembly concludes there should be five pounds of tobacco per poll levied through the colony.

Every master of a family and every freeman that is to pay five pounds of tobacco per poll for the defraying of public charges shall bring the same unto the houses of the burgesses of the plantations within two days after notice thereof given unto them.

1629. Act IX. It is thought fit that all those that work in the ground of what quality or condition soever shall pay tithes to the ministers.[2]

---

[1] It is interesting to note a similar section to limit tobacco planting because the market had become gutted in 1666.

[2] In 1623 the General Assembly ordained that there should be uniformity in the churches as near as may be possible to the canons in England, and that all persons yield ready obedience unto them under pain of censure, and that whosoever absents himself from divine service on Sunday without an allowed excuse shall forfeit a pound of tobacco.

1642. Act I. All freemen that are hired servants shall pay their own tithes and duties. Divers poor people that have been of very long continuance in this country and are disabled by sickness or age, are exempt from all public charges, except ministers' and parish duties.

Ministers' allowances are enacted and confirmed to be ten pounds of tobacco per poll and a bushel of corn per poll for all tithable persons, that is to say, as well for all youths of sixteen years of age and upwards, as also for all Negro women of the age of sixteen years.

1644. Act VIII. It is declared that because there shall be no scruple or invasion as to who are and who are not tithable, it is resolved by the General Assembly that all Negro men and women, and all other men, from the age of sixteen to sixty shall be adjudged tithable.

1645. Act X. Juries shall be chosen of the most able men of the country.

1645. Act XV. Whereas, the ancient and usual taxing of all people of this colony by the poll equally has been found inconvenient and has become insupportable for the poorer sort to bear, it is enacted that all public levies be raised by equal proportions out of the visible estate of the colony; the proportion to be as follows: one hundred acres of land at 04 pounds of tobacco, one cow three years old at 04; horses, mares and geldings at 32 a piece, a breeding sheep at 04, a breeding goat at 02, a tithable person at 20.

1646. Act XX. This act sets a penalty on what freemen soever having lawful summons of the time and place for election of burgesses shall not make repair accordingly, servants being exempt.

1648. Act VI. The act of the Assembly which ordained all levies hereafter should be raised from lands, horses, mares, sheep and from tithable persons is hereby repealed, it being only intended for the better support of the war, and instead thereof, it is enacted all levies shall be hereafter raised upon tithable persons by the poll.

1649. Act II. Whereas, notwithstanding the yearly importation of people into the colony, the number of tithables is rather diminished than augmented, it is enacted that all male servants imported hereafter into the colony of what age soever they shall be brought into the lists and liable to pay county levies, except such as are natives and such as are imported free either by their parents or otherwise, who are exempt from levies, being under the age of sixteen years.

1654. Act VII. The persons who shall be elected to serve in the Assembly shall be such and no other than as are persons of known integrity and of good conversation and of the age of twenty-one years. All housekeepers, whether freeholders, leaseholders, or otherwise tenants, shall be capable to elect burgesses. A penalty of 400 pounds of tobacco for voting if not qualified is provided, but one person only in a family is to vote.[3]

1655. Act XVI. Whereas, we conceive it something hard and unagreeable to reason that any person shall pay equal taxes and yet have no votes in elections, it is enacted that so much

---

[3]It would appear that this is the first abridgment of the right of suffrage in Virginia; apparently all freemen were previously voters. Note 1655, XVI especially.

of the act for choosing burgesses be repealed as excludes freemen from votes; provided always that they fairly give their
votes and not in a tumultous way.

1657. Act XLVI.   It is enacted that all male servants hereafter imported into this colony of whatever age shall be liable
to pay county levies, and all Negroes imported, whether male
or female, and Indian servants, male or female, however procured, being sixteen years of age; such Christians only to be
excepted as are natives of this country, or such as are imported free, who are exempt because under sixteen years of
age.

1657. Act CXVIII.   Citizenship is conferred on all aliens
and strangers who have inhabited the country four years and
have a firm resolution to make this country their place of residence, provided they take the oath of fidelity to be true to the
government.

1659. Act XVI.   Dutch and all strangers of Christian nations
are allowed free trade if they give bond and pay impost of
ten shillings per hogshead laid upon all tobacco exported to
any foreign dominions; always provided that if the Dutch
or other foreigners shall import any Negro slaves they, the
said Dutch or other foreigners, shall for the tobacco really
produced by the sale of the said Negroes, pay only the impost
of two shillings per hogshead, the like being paid by our
own nation.[4]

1662. Act XIII.   Whereas, divers persons purchase women
servants to work in the ground to avoid the payment of levies,
it is enacted that women servants whose common employ-

---

[4]This appears to be the first use of *Negro slave* in Virginia legislation.

ment is working in the crops shall be tithable and shall be named by every master in his list of tithables, under penalty.

1663. Act VII. Tithable persons concealed by their master are to be forfeited to the informer, but if any concealed person being a servant has less than a year to serve, or is a freeman, then for every such person the master of the family shall forfeit 1,000 pounds of tobacco, provided that women servants be excepted; whether they are tithable or not is referred to the county courts.[5]

1668. Act VII. Negro women though permitted to enjoy their freedom, yet ought not in all respects to be admitted to a full fruition of the exemptions of the English and are still liable to the payment of taxes.[6]

1670. Act III. Whereas the usual way of choosing burgesses by the votes of all persons who have served their time as freemen, who having little interest in the country do often make tumults at the election than by their discretion in their votes provide for the conservation thereof by making choice of persons fitly qualified, and whereas, the laws of England grant a voice in such election only to such as by their estates have interest enough to tie them to the public good, it is enacted that none but freeholders and housekeepers shall have a voice in the election of any burgesses.[7]

---

[5] In September of the same year a grand committee of the House concluded, and it was assented to by the governor that the most equal way of paying taxes is by a levy on land and not upon heads. It is amusing to read that in the same year the Assembly considered whether it would not be more profitable to purchase a state house "than continue forever at the expense, accompanied with the dishonor of all our laws being made and over judgments given in ale-houses."

[6] There had been free Negroes in Virginia long before 1668, but this seems to be the first direct reference in the law to them.

[7] This act for the first time limits the elective franchise to freeholders and by its terms includes emancipated Negro freeholders.

1676. Act VII. The act which forbids freemen to have votes
in the election of burgesses is repealed, and they may be admitted with freeholders and housekeepers to vote as formerly.[8]

1677. Instruction of Charles, Rex, for Sir William Berkely,
Governor of the Virginia colony: You shall take care that
members of the Assembly be elected only by freeholders, as
being more agreeable to the custom of England.

1680. Act VII. This act deems it too hard and severe for
children, Christians as well as slaves, imported into the colony
to be liable to taxes before they are capable of working. It
is accordingly enacted that Negroes shall not be tithable until
twelve years of age and no Christian servant before fourteen
years, former laws or customs notwithstanding.

1682. Act II. Indian women servants sold to the English are
to pay levies in like manner as Negro women.

1699. Act II. It is enacted that no person shall vote for
burgesses to serve in the General Assembly, except freeholders, and it is the true meaning and intent of this act that
no women sole or covert, infants under twenty-one years, or
recusant convict being freeholders shall have a voice in the
election of burgesses.[9]

1699. Act IV. No person shall be capable to serve as a juror
in the general court except a freeholder, whose lands and
goods are visibly worth one hundred pounds sterling; in the

---

[8]From Bacon's laws.
[9]Hening's marginal heading reads "no Popish recusant is entitled to vote." Negro
freeholders are not mentioned in the exceptions. Does this mean they voted until 1723?
See 1723, Chapter IV, post. A recusant was a person who refused to attend the Anglican
Church; the term was applied especially to Roman Catholics.

county court jurors must have estates to the value of at least fifty pounds sterling.[10]

1699. Act XII. Whereas, the state house of this dominion has been burnt down, and as a more suitable expedient cannot be found for avoiding a levy upon the poll for building the same, a duty of fifteen and twenty shillings, respectively, is placed on servants and slaves imported into his majesty's colony and dominion, and no servant or Negro shall be put ashore until the duty is paid. It is enacted that the act be in force three years.

1701. Act V. Acts levying an imposition on liquors, servants and slaves for building the capitol, having proved very advantageous and useful, are continued in force to December 23, 1703.

1705. Act VII. It is enacted that all male persons of the age of sixteen years and upward, and all Negro, mulatto, and Indian women of sixteen years, not being free shall be tithable or chargeable for defraying the public, county, and parish charges in this her majesty's colony and dominion, excepting such only as the county court and vestry for reasons in charity shall think fit to excuse. Every master or mistress shall, under penalty, by a list cause to be delivered to the justice the name of all tithable persons belonging to his or her family.

1723. Chapter IV. All free Negroes, mulattoes, and Indians (except tributary Indians to this government), male and female above sixteen years of age, and all wives of such, shall be deemed tithables.

---

[10] In 1748 the value of the estate was estimated in "current money."

No free Negro or Indian whatsoever shall hereafter have any vote at any election.

1732. Chapter III. The General Assembly humbly represents to his majesty, that the duty laid upon liquors is not sufficient to defray the expenses of the government and no other duty can be laid without oppression, than one on slaves imported to be paid by buyers, and his majesty is beseeched that a duty be levied of five pounds per cent on the amount of each such purchase. An exception is made if the slave is exported within twelve months, but as it is very easy to convey slaves into the province of North Carolina and bring them back again and thereby evade the payment of duty, it is enacted that no drawback shall be allowed for slaves carried or exported by land or water into North Carolina.[11]

1736. Chapter I. The act recites former acts laying import duties on liquors and slaves and re-enacts them with amendments for better securing of the duties; in case of slaves dying within forty days the duty to be remitted.

1740. Chapter II. To encourage enlistment, an additional duty is laid on all slaves imported; out of the money so raised, the sum of 500 pounds shall be paid for the support of persons enlisted in his majesty's service in this colony; a deserter who escapes the punishment of the martial law is to be sold to the highest bidder for ready money, as a servant for five years.

1748. Chapter XXI. All male persons of the age of sixteen years and over and all Negro and Indian women of the same

[11]In 1734 this duty being found in no way burdensome it was continued for four years, again in 1738, 1742, and 1745. Duty on imported slaves was extended seven years in 1757, and again in 1759. Because "burdensome" it was repealed in 1760 but later revived.

age, except tributary Indians, and all wives of free Negroes and Indians are tithable and chargeable for defraying the public and parish levies, except such as the county courts for charitable reasons shall excuse.

Owners of imported children, being servants or slaves, shall bring them to court and have their age adjudged and recorded.

1752. Chapter I. The debts contracted during the late war with France and also for rebuilding the capitol are still unpaid, and so for the space of four years the duty of five pounds per cent on the amount of each purchase of any slave imported into the colony for sale, from any port or place whatsoever, shall be revived and paid.[12]

The importer or seller shall, after the sale of the slaves, deliver to the treasurer of Virginia under oath an account of the slaves sold, the prices for which the slaves were sold, whether for sterling, current money or tobacco, or other commodity, and the buyer shall pay the duty according to the valuation.

If any slave shall die within forty days after purchase, the buyer is discharged from the payment of duty.

1762. Chapter I. No woman, infant under twenty-one years of age, recusant, convict, person convicted in Great Britain or Ireland during the time for which he is transported, nor any free Negro, mulatto, or Indian, although such persons are freeholders, shall have a vote.

1769. Act XXXVII. The law which declared all free Negro, mulatto and Indian women and all wives of free Negroes to be tithable is found very burdensome to such Negroes, and

---

[12]In 1755 the duty was placed at 10 per cent: in 1759 a duty of 20 per cent on slaves imported from Maryland, North Carolina and other places in America was laid.

moreover derogatory of the rights of free-born subjects. It is
therefore enacted that all free Negro and Indian women,
and all wives, other than slaves, of free Negroes and Indians
are exempt from being tithables, and from the payment of
public or parish levies.

1776. Chapter II.   Whereas, there are within this Commonwealth great numbers of dissenters from the church established by law who have been heretofore taxed for its support
contrary to the principles of reason and justice, for remedy
whereof, and that equal liberty as well religious as civil may
be universally extended, it is enacted that all dissenters shall
be totally free and exempt from all levies, taxes and impo-
sitions toward supporting the church.[13]

But vestries shall be required to levy on all tithables as well
dissenters as others, all salaries and arrears of salaries as may
be due to ministers for services to January 1, 1776; moreover, to make such assessments on all tithables as will enable the vestries to comply with their legal parochial engagements already entered, and lastly to continue such future
provisions for the poor as they have by law been accustomed
to make.

And every master or owner of a family shall deliver a list
of the names and number of all tithable persons abiding in
or belonging to his family on June 9, last.

1779. Chapter I.   A tax of five pounds per poll shall be paid
for all Negro and mulatto servants and slaves, but when any
slave is through old age or infirmity incapable of labor, the
tax may be discontinued.

[13]In 1631 the Virginia Assembly had enacted that a penalty of one shilling was to be
levied for every time a person was absent from church having no lawful or reasonable
excuse. In 1785 it was declared that no man should be compelled to frequent or support
any religious worship, place or minister.

1779. Chapter LV.   All white persons born within this Commonwealth and all who have resided here two years, all who shall migrate into the state, other than alien enemies, and give proof that they intend to reside therein and give assurance of fidelity to the Commonwealth, and infants whose father if living, otherwise their mother, migrate here, shall be deemed citizens.[14]

1779. Chapter XXIV.   This act to raise money for carrying on the Revolutionary War provides that the following additional taxes shall be laid, a poll tax on all free male persons above twenty-one years of age, and on all white servants, except apprentices, to be paid by the owner the sum of three pounds by the poll, except soldiers and others exempt, and by the owners of slaves the sum of four pounds by the poll, except old slaves; and on coaches and chariots, the sum of forty pounds each.[15]

1780. Chapter X.   An act for calling in the continental money and for emitting new bills lays a further tax in the paper money of this state on money, white male tithables, servants, cattle, carriages, spirits, marriage licenses, etc., (slaves do not seem to be included).[16]

1781. Chapter XL.   An act for establishing permanent revenue provides that there be a tax of one pound for every hundred pounds of the valuation of lands and lots, ten shillings on every free male person above twenty-one years, and also on slaves to be paid by their owners, except those exempt by age or infirmity, two shillings for every horse, three pence for cattle,

---

[14]Taken from the May session of this year.
[15]Taken from the October session of this year.
[16]Taken from the May session laws.

five shillings per wheel on coaches, also fifty pounds for billiard tables, five pounds for every ordinary license.

1782. Chapter XXI. Liberated slaves neglecting to pay tax levies may be hired out by the sheriff long enough to raise the taxes.

1782. Chapter L. An act for calling in and redeeming military certificates places additional taxes on lands, free male persons, slaves, horses, etc.[17]

1783. Chapter XI. Money arising from the tax on slaves shall be applied toward the payment of this state's debt due to the army; and also for making good to Congress any deficiency in the state's interest on debts of the United States so as to make good to Congress the annual sum of $400,000.

1787. Chapter I. The poll tax on free males above twenty-one years and the tax on young slaves are repealed. But it is reasonable that slaves above twelve years should pay taxes, and a tax of ten shillings shall therefore be paid for the same.

1792. Chapter 48. Artisans, mechanics and handicraft tradesmen migrating into the state are wholly exempt from the payment of tax on tools or implements of trade and are exempt for five years from all taxes, except land taxes.[18]

1793. Chapter 14. Hereafter every grand juror shall be also a citizen of this Commonwealth, in addition to other requisites.

---

[17]There were other similar acts in 1782 and 1784.
[18]Repealed in 1826, Chapter 5.

1796. Chapter 3. A tax of 25 cents per $100.00 of value in land is laid; and for every slave above twelve years, except the infirm, 28 cents.[19]

1814. Chapter I. This act imposes taxes on land, property and slaves, and makes all male free Negroes above sixteen years subject to a poll tax of $1.50, except those bound out as apprentices.

1814. Chapter II. Correct tax lists, set down separately, shall be made of all male free Negroes and mulattoes above sixteen years of age. The poll tax on free Negroes shall be collected by sheriffs in the same manner and at the same times as they collect taxes on the taxable property of the Commonwealth.

1814. Chapter XX. In case any free Negro or mulatto shall neglect in any year to pay all taxes, poor rates, and levies, he may be hired out for so long a time as will raise the said taxes, provided sufficient cannot be raised on his estate, and provided the Negro has been first summoned to show cause, if any, against making such order.[20]

1818. Chapter I. Public taxes for 1818 shall be on lands for every $100.00 value, agreeable to the equalizing law of 1782, 75 cents for houses in town, $3.00 for every one hundred dollars yearly rent; for slaves above twelve years old, 70 cents;[21] for every stallion or jackass, twice the price at which such stallion or jackass covers a mare by the season.

---

[19]In 1802 the tax was raised to 48 cents on land, and 44 cents on slaves. In succeeding years the land tax was 64 cents and 85 cents for every land value; on slaves 59 cents and 79 cents. In 1815 the tax on slave children between 9 and 12 years was 50 cents.

[20]Passed in October.

[21]The tax on slaves was levied regularly but varied from year to year. In 1831, '32, '33, '35, for instance, it was 25 cents and in 1860 and 1862, $1.20.

1818. Chapter XLII. The right of suffrage is to be enjoyed by every male citizen of the Commonwealth aged twenty-one years, other than free Negroes or mulattoes, or such as have refused to give assurance of fidelity to the Commonwealth, possessed of twenty-five acres of land, with a house, twelve foot square, or fifty acres of unimproved land, or a lot with a house thereon in the city.

Any elector qualified failing to attend an annual election of delegates, or of a senator, and if a poll be given to offer his vote, shall pay one-fourth of his portion of all such levies and taxes as shall be assessed in his county the ensuing year.

1820. Chapter XXXII. It shall be lawful to hire out free Negroes and mulattoes for the payment of their taxes and levies, provided that no one shall be hired for a less sum than 8 cents a day.

1830. Constitution of Virginia. Article III, Section 14. The right of suffrage is conferred on those white males of twenty-one years and upward being qualified under the former constitution and every such citizen having an estate in land of $25.00, and every such citizen who for twelve months has been a housekeeper and head of a family and has been assessed and has actually paid part of the revenue of the Commonwealth within the preceding year, except persons of unsound mind, paupers, and those convicted of an infamous offense.

1848. Criminal Code. Chapter 120; Chapter XXI, Section 5. No person shall be capable to be of a jury for the trial of a felony unless he be a freeholder over the age of twenty-one years and possessed of a visible estate of the value of $300.00 at least.

1850. Chapter 6. The sum of $30,000.00 is hereby appropriated to be paid annually for five years for transporting and subsisting free persons of color who shall embark for Liberia on the Western Coast of Africa, $25.00 a person to be allowed for persons above ten years of age.

It is further enacted that an annual tax of one dollar shall be levied upon every male free Negro of the age of twenty-one and under fifty-five years, collected as other taxes upon free Negroes are collected. The fund arising shall be applied to the removal of Negroes from the Commonwealth in addition to the appropriation herein made.[22]

1850-1851. Constitution of Virginia. Qualification of voters: Every white male citizen of the Commonwealth of the age of twenty-one years, who has been a resident of the state two years, except those of unsound mind, paupers, or who have been convicted of an infamous offense.

1852. Chapter I. An act concerning commissioners of the revenue states each person of full age and sound mind, not a married woman, shall list the personal property subject to taxation of which such person is the owner. From the lists thus furnished, the commissioner of the revenue shall make accurate statements which shall set forth: the number of white male inhabitants who have attained twenty-one years; the number of slaves who have attained the age of twelve years; the number of horses, mules, asses, etc., and the value thereof. The commissioner shall also ascertain the number

---

[22] For tax appropriations made for transporting condemned slaves see Chapter VII.

of free male persons above sixteen years of age and the number of slaves above the age who are subject to county levies. He shall also ascertain the number of male free Negroes between the ages of twenty-one and fifty-five years.

1852. Chapter 17. Taxes imposed for the year 1852-53: on every slave, above twelve years, 54 cents; on every male free Negro between twenty-one and fifty-five years, $1.00; on every white male inhabitant who has attained the age of twenty-one years, 36 cents; on all land and lots with improvements thereon, 18 cents on every $100.00 of value; on incomes, fees, or salaries, varying assessments, etc.

1853. Chapter 27. All free white male persons, who are twenty-one years of age and not over sixty, shall be liable to serve as jurors, with certain exemptions.

1860. Chapter 3. This act places on land a tax of 40 cents per hundred, on slaves over twelve years of age, whether exempt from county levy for bodily infirmity or not, a tax of $1.20; on every male free Negro of twenty-one years, 80 cents, and on every white male, 80 cents; on incomes above $250.00, certain taxes; on every license to buy or sell slaves for others on commission or for profit, $10.00; on the yearly income derived from such business an additional tax of ½ of 1 per cent, etc.

1862. Chapter I. This act imposing taxes for the support of the government lays increased taxes on lands and lots, personal property, male free Negroes of the age of twenty-one years, (but no tax to be collected on free Negroes for the colonization fund), white males, public bonds, bank dividends, incomes, toll bridges, inheritances, corporations, licenses for persons engaged as agents for hiring Negroes set at $75.00. The number of slaves and the value thereof shall be listed and taxed according to value.

1863. Chapter I. Virginia tax on male free Negroes is placed at $2.00, and on white males at $2.00.

Slaves shall be taxed according to their value, but taxes on slaves carried away by the public enemy, or escaping to the public owner may be exonerated.

1863. Chapter 64. This law, passed by the extra session of the General Assembly meeting at Wheeling, places a tax on every slave above twelve years, whether exempt from county levy by bodily infirmity or not, of 90 cents; on male free Negroes above twenty-one years of age, 60 cents; on white males, 60 cents.

1866. Chapter 3. The tax upon every male person not exempt for bodily infirmity is placed at 28 cents.

1867. Chapter 46. On January 9th the Assembly ratifies the proposed 14th Amendment to the Constitution of the United States stating that all persons born or naturalized in the United States and subject to the jurisdiction thereof are citizens of the United States and of the state wherein they reside; and no state shall abridge the privileges of citizens of the United States, nor deprive any person of life, liberty or property without due process of law, nor deny any person the equal protection of the law.

1867–1870. Constitution of Virginia. Article I, Section 19. Neither slavery nor involuntary servitude, except as lawful imprisonment may constitute such, shall exist in the state.

Section 20. All citizens of the state are hereby declared
to possess equal civil and political rights and public privileges.[23]

Article III. Section 1. Every male person twenty-one years
of age, resident of the state one year, of the county, city or
town, three months, who has paid the capitation tax for the
preceding year, shall be entitled to vote. United States soldiers and sailors stationed in Virginia, idiots, lunatics, persons
convicted of felony are excepted.[24]

Section 3. All persons entitled to vote or hold office, and
none other, shall be eligible to sit as jurors.

1869. Chapter I. This act ratifies the fifteenth amendment
to the Federal Constitution, which provides that the rights
of citizens of the United States to vote, shall not be abridged
on account of race, color, or previous condition of servitude.

1869. Chapter 2. This act ratifies the fourteenth amendment to the Constitution of the United States.

1870. Chapter 46. This act provides for a general registration of all male citizens of twenty-one years, citizens of the
United States, resident of the state one year, of the county
or city, three months. The list of voters, white and colored,
shall be kept in separate books.

1870. Chapter 76. This act provides for general elections,
and every male citizen of the United States, twenty-one

[23]1873. The Virginia Code of this year states that in 1870 Virginia was admitted to
representation in Congress having ratified the 14th and 15th amendments to the United
States Constitution and adopted a new constitution of republican state goverment, on
condition that the constitution of Virginia shall never be amended to deprive citizens
of the United States of the right to vote who are entitled to vote by the Constitution here
recognized except under laws applicable to all the inhabitants of the state.
[24]The capitation tax clause was adopted in 1876, was omitted in the amendment of
1882, but later re-adopted.

years of age, resident of the state for twelve months and three months in the city, who is registered, shall be entitled to vote; idiots, lunatics, felons excluded.

1870. Chapter 358. This act amends the previous citizenship law of the state and defines citizens to be all persons born in this state or persons born in any other state of the Union who may become residents of this state and all naturalized resident aliens.

1871. Chapter 57. All male citizens twenty-one to sixty years of age, entitled to vote and hold office, shall be liable to serve as jurors, except persons convicted of scandalous offense, or those guilty of gross immorality. The judge shall prepare a list of inhabitants as he shall think well qualified to serve, being persons of sound judgment.

1874. Chapter I. The General Assembly recognizes the 14th amendment to the Constitution of the United States as a part of that instrument and desires in good faith to abide by its provisions as expounded by the Supreme Court of the United States. That tribunal recently held that it is only the privileges and immunities of the citizens of the United States that are placed under the protection of the Constitution and privileges of the citizens of the state are not intended to have any additional protection.

The bill before Congress, known as the civil rights bill, is in violation of this amendment. It is an infringement on the constitutional powers of the state; it is sectional in its operation and injurious alike to the white and colored population of the Southern States; its enforced application in these states will prove destructive of their systems of education, arrest the

enlightenment of the colored population (in whose improvement the people of Virginia feel a lively interest), and produce continual irritation between the races.

1877. Chapter 271. This act is for the purpose of enforcing
the constitutional amendments restricting the right of suffrage to citizens who shall have paid to the state before
the day of election, the capitation tax required for the previous year. In reference to the required registration, it is
stated that the registrar shall register all male citizens twenty-
one years of age who have resided in the state twelve months
and the county or city three months, with the exception of
United States army and navy men, idiots and lunatics, persons convicted of felony, those who have fought duels, etc.

1896. Chapter 398. It shall be lawful for any political
party in the County of Henrico, in this state, previous to
any general election held for the purpose of electing any
state, county or federal officers, should it desire so to do, to
hold a primary election upon such rules as may be prescribed
by the local county committee of such party. Any person
voting or attempting to vote at such primary elections contrary to the rules governing same, or fraudulently registering for the purpose of voting, or who is not a member of the
party holding the election, is guilty of a misdemeanor.[25]

1900. Chapter 226. All railroad companies running by
steam, within this state, are required to furnish separate
coaches for the transportation of white and colored passengers. There shall be no difference in the quality, conveni-

---

[25]Similar acts were passed for other counties. Present Virginia law contains provisions
relative to party primaries but courts have held Negroes cannot be excluded from party
membership.

ences and accommodations in the cars. Failure of any railroad company to comply with this act is a misdemeanor. Passengers refusing to occupy the car to which they are assigned by the conductor may be put off the train. Failure of the conductor to carry out the provisions of this act is a misdemeanor. When any coach for either race is filled, the conductor may set apart a portion of a car assigned to passengers of the other race. This act does not apply to nurses, railroad employees, officers in charge of prisoners, passengers in a caboose on a freight train, Pullman cars, express trains doing local business.[26]

1900. Chapter 312. This is an act to provide for the separate accommodation without discrimination in quality and convenience, of white and colored passengers in the sitting, sleeping and eating apartments of steamboats plying in the waters within the jurisdiction of the Commonwealth, and to provide police powers to captains and other officers to enforce the law.

1901. Chapter 198. The Richmond Passenger and Power Company is required to provide separate accommodations, plainly designated, for white and colored passengers, on its line between 29th and P Streets in the City of Richmond and Seven Pines in the County of Henrico.

1902. Chapter 64. This act vests conductors and motormen on street cars in the counties of the state with police powers and authorizes them to carry arms hid from common observation while on duty.

---

[26]This act as amended was repealed in 1904, by Chapter 253 but by Chap. 609, 1904 on public service corporations, separation of the races is fully covered and may be found in the Code of 1936 in sections 3962 et seq.

1902. Chapter 454. This is an act requiring the Richmond and Petersburg Railway Company to provide separate accommodations for white and colored passengers, and conferring upon conductors and motormen powers of conservators of the peace and policemen.

1902. Constitution of Virginia.[27] Article II, Section 18. Every male citizen of the United States, twenty-one years of age, resident of the state two years, county or city one year, precinct thirty days, who has been registered and has paid his poll taxes, shall be entitled to vote.

Section 19. At the registration every such male citizen of the United States shall be entitled to register, if prior to the adoption of this Constitution he served in time of war in the army or navy of the United States, or the Confederate States, or is a son of such a person, or owns property on which he has paid state taxes aggregating at least $1.00 for the preceding year, or is a person able to read any section of the Constitution, or able to give a reasonable explanation thereof.

Section 20. After 1904 every male citizen in order to register shall personally pay all state poll taxes assessed against him for the three years next preceding that in which he offers to register; or if he comes of age at such time that no poll tax shall have been assessable against him, has paid $1.50 in satisfaction of the first year's poll tax assessable against him.

Unless physically unable, he shall make application to register in his own handwriting.

Section 21. Poll taxes for three years shall be personally paid at least six months prior to the election.

[27] In 1902-03 the Assembly passed legislation conforming to the constitution.

Section 22. Ex-soldiers are not required to pay poll tax as a prerequisite to register, etc.

Section 30. The Assembly may prescribe a property qualification of not exceeding $250.00.

1903. Chapter 327. Any person denied registration shall have the right to appeal without payment of tax or giving security for costs to the circuit court of the county or corporation court of the city.

1904. Chapter 85. Any corporation, its agents, or conductors operating in this state sleeping, dining, palace, or compartment cars on railroads, are empowered to reject and refuse admittance to any and all persons to enter and ride in such cars, when in the discretion of the corporation or its employees it may be advisable to do so.

1904. Chapter 115. Qualifications and disqualifications of voters: Every male citizen, twenty-one years old, who has been a resident of the state two years, of the county or city one year, who has been duly registered and has paid his state poll tax, and is otherwise qualified.

The following are excluded from registering and voting: idiots, insane, paupers, and those convicted of crime, those who have fought a duel. No soldier or seaman of the United States gains a residence because stationed in the state, inmates of charitable institutions or students in institutions of learning do not gain or lose a residence by reason of location, or sojourn in such institutions.

1912. Chapter 157. Whereas, the preservation of the public morals, public health and public order in the cities and towns of this Commonwealth is endangered by the residence of white and colored people in close proximity to one another, it is enacted that in cities and towns where this act is adopted, the entire area within the corporate limits shall be divided into "segregation districts." It shall be unlawful for any colored person to move into a white district, or a white person to move into a colored district. This act does not preclude persons of either race employed as servants by persons of the other race from residing on the premises of the employer.[28]

1918. Chapter 301. In the penitentiary the races shall be kept separate.

1920. Chapter I. Jury commissioners to be appointed by judges shall be persons competent to serve as jurors and shall be men of intelligence, morality and integrity.

These commissioners are to prepare a list of the inhabitants well qualified to serve as jurors and not exempt. The commissioners must take oath to select only persons whom they believe to be of good repute for intelligence and honesty, and in all selections endeavor to promote the impartial administration of justice.[29]

1926. Chapter 569. It shall be the duty of any person, firm or institution conducting any public hall, theatre, motion picture, show, or any place of public entertainment or assemblage which is attended by both white and colored

---

[28] By the Code of 1936 Virginia cities are permitted to adopt segregation ordinances although the Supreme Court of the United States has declared them to be unconstitutional.

[29] Previously the judges themselves made the jury lists; a commission is used today. Persons above sixty years are not now disqualified from jury service but may claim exemption. The exemptions include many officers and professional people, persons who contribute at least $25.00 a year to the Virginia National Guard, etc.

persons, to separate the white race and the colored race, and to set apart and designate in each public place of public entertainment or assemblage, certain seats to be occupied by white persons and certain by colored persons. Failure to comply is a misdemeanor and the one guilty may be fined from $100.00 to $500.00 for each offense. The one who fails to take the seat assigned is also guilty of a misdemeanor and may be ejected from the place, and if admission has been paid, he shall not be entitled to a return of any part of the same.

1928. Virginia Constitution of 1920, as revised. Article II, Section 18. Every citizen of the United States, twenty-one years of age, who has been a resident of the state one year and of the county or city six months, and of the precinct thirty days, and has registered and personally paid his poll taxes, may vote. Certain widows, idiots, insane persons, paupers, persons convicted of crime, whose disabilities have not been removed are excepted.

Sections 20–21. Poll taxes for three years must be paid at least six months prior to voting or registering. Application to register must be made in one's own handwriting without aid, stating name, age, occupation and so on. Also the applicant must answer any other question affecting his qualifications as an elector. Soldiers and widows of soldiers are not required to pay poll taxes as a prerequisite to registering.[30]

1928. Chapter 45. The Tax Code lays a capitation tax of $1.50 per annum on every resident of the state twenty-one years of age.

---

[30]Laws in harmony with the Constitution have been passed. The following general classes are excluded from voting in Virginia: idiots, insane persons and paupers, persons convicted of crime whose disabilities have not been removed, etc.

1930. Chapter 128. All passenger motor vehicles shall separate white and colored passengers in their motor busses and set apart in each bus a portion thereof or certain seats to be occupied by white passengers and certain by colored passengers. Failure to comply is a misdemeanor.

There shall be no difference or discrimination in the quality or convenience of the accommodation provided for the two races.

Drivers shall be special policemen and have all the powers of conservators of the peace in the enforcement of this act. Persons who fail to occupy the seats assigned are guilty of a misdemeanor and may be ejected and shall not be entitled to the return of any part of their fare.

CHAPTER VII

Criminal Law and the Negro

1692. Act III. This is an act for the more speedy prosecution of slaves committing capital offenses and is the first law constituting a tribunal expressly for the trial of slaves. It provides for committing a Negro or slave who has committed a capital offense to the common gaol, well-laden with irons. A special commission shall cause the offender to be arraigned and take for evidence the confession[1] of the party, or the oaths of two witnesses, or of one with pregnant circumstances, without the solemnity of jury.

It is further enacted that horses, cattle and hogs marked by any slave and not converted to his use by the owner shall be converted by the owner to the use of the poor of the parish.

1699. Act VI. The penalty for the first offense of hog stealing by a Negro or a slave is set at thirty lashes on the bare back, well laid on; for the second offense, two hours in the pillory with boths ears nailed thereto, at the expiration of the two hours the ears are to be cut off close by the nails.

1699. Act VII. The penalty for killing deer between the first of February and the first of July, or buying them from Indians, is a fine of 500 pounds of tobacco, provided always that any slave or other servant incapable of paying the penalty shall receive on his bare back thirty lashes, well laid on.

---

[1]Blackstone calls confessions the "most suspicious of all testimony." In general, care should always be taken to safeguard the free and voluntary character of a confession.

1705. Chapter XI. It is provided that a slave's master may make defence for a slave accused of an offense, satisfied by death or loss of member; the justices which sit at the trial shall put a valuation in money on the condemned slave and the Assembly shall make a suitable allowance to the owner of the slave.

1705. Chapter XIV. It is enacted that if any person shall steal any hog or pig, for the first offense he shall receive on his bare back twenty-five lashes or pay ten pounds current money; and if a Negro or Indian, thirty-nine lashes well laid on, at the common whipping post, and moreover shall pay 400 pounds of tobacco for each hog. And if any person shall offend the second time, he shall stand in the pillory and have both ears nailed thereto, and at the end of two hours have the ears cut loose from the nails. And for the third offense he shall be adjudged a felon and shall suffer death.

The master or owner of a hogstealing servant, by indenture or custom, shall pay the fines and shall be satisfied for the same by the service of the servant at the rate of 150 pounds of tobacco for one month's service.

If the offender is a slave, the owner shall pay 200 pounds of tobacco to the owner of the hog.

1705. Chapter XIX. In Section 31 it is stated that Popish recusants, convicts, Negroes, mulattoes, and Indian servants, and others not being Christians, shall be incapable to be witnesses in any cases whatsoever.

1705. Chapter XLIV. In Section 34 it is declared that if any slave resist his master, or owner, or other person, by his or her order correcting such slave, and shall happen to be killed in such correction, it shall not be accounted felony; but the master, owner, and every such other person so giving correction shall be free and acquit of all punishment and accusation for the same, as if such incident had never happened: And also if any Negro, mulatto, or Indian, bond or free, shall at any time lift his or her hand in opposition against any Christian, not being Negro, mulatto, or Indian, he or she so offending, shall for every such offense, proved by the oath of the party, receive on his or her bare back thirty lashes, well laid on.

1723. Chapter IV. Every slave committing a capital crime shall be publicly arraigned and tried, and for evidence the confession of the offender, the oath of one or more credible witnesses, or the testimony of Negroes, mulattoes, or Indians, bond or free, with pregnant circumstances, may be taken, without the solemnity of a jury. If a Negro or Indian, not being a Christian, give false testimony every such offender shall, without further trial, be ordered by the court to have one ear nailed to the pillory one hour and then have the said ear cut off, and thereafter the other ear nailed and cut off; moreover, to receive thirty-nine lashes, well laid on, on the bare back.

And for preventing all doubts upon the construction of this or any other act of the Assembly touching the death of slaves under correction, or lawful punishment, it is enacted that if any slave shall happen to die by means of dismembering by court order, or by any stroke or blow during his or her correction by his or her owner, for any offense committed, or for or by reason of any accidental blow whatsoever given by the owner, no person concerned in the dismem-

bering or accidental homicide shall undergo any prosecution
or punishment, unless it shall be proved that such slave was
killed wilfully; neither shall any person who shall be indicted
for the murder of any slave and shall be found guilty of
manslaughter incur any punishment for the offense or misfortune.

1732. Chapter VII. Acts of Parliament of England taking
away benefit of clergy[2] are herewith adopted in respect to
principal and accessories standing mute and challenging a
greater number of the jury than the law allows; clergy is to
be allowed to women as to men, and they shall suffer the same
punishment as men.

When Negroes and Indians are convicted of any offense
within the benefit of clergy judgment of death shall not be
given but they shall be burnt in the hand in open court and
suffer such other corporal punishment as the court may deem
fit, except where the conviction is for manslaughter, breaking and entering in the night time or day time, and taking
away goods of the value of five shillings; where he has had
once the benefit of this act, a Negro shall suffer death.

And whereas, Negroes and Indians have lately frequently
been allowed to give testimony as lawful witnesses, when
they have professed themselves to be Christians, and being
able to give some account of the principles of the Christian
religion: But forasmuch as they are people of such base and
corrupt natures, that their testimony cannot certainly be de-
pended upon, and some juries have altogether rejected their

---

[2]Benefit of clergy originally meant the exemption of clergymen from the secular courts.
Afterward it came to mean an exemption from the punishment of death and was extended
to "clerks" or those who could read. The privilege greatly mitigated the criminal law,
but led to such abuses that Parliament began to enact that certain felonies should be without benefit of clergy. Finally by St. 7, George IV, the exemption was altogether abolished.
By act of Congress 1790, crimes against the United States were not to have benefit of
clergy.

evidence, and others have given full credit thereto: For preventing the mischiefs that may possibly happen by admitting such precarious evidence, it is enacted that no Negro, mulatto, or Indian, either slave or free, shall hereafter be sworn as a witness, except upon the trial of a slave, for a capital offense.

1748. Chapter XIV. In Section 25 it is stated that if any person shall steal a Negro or Indian slave he is a felon and shall suffer death without benefit of clergy.

1748. Chapter XXXVIII. Whereas, under pretence of practising physic, Negroes have prepared medicine by which many persons have been murdered or have languished, it is enacted that if any Negro, or other slave, shall prepare, exhibit, or administer any medicine whatsoever, he shall be guilty of felony and suffer death without benefit of clergy, but clergy may be allowed if it is shown that there was no ill intent; also medicines may be administered with the consent of the owner.

Section 6. The trial of a Negro shall be on confession or oath of one or more witnesses, but if the court is of divided opinion, the Negro shall be acquitted.

Section 8. When judgment of death is passed, ten days must elapse before execution, except in cases of conspiracy, insurrection, or rebellion.[3]

Section 11. Negroes are to testify only in the trial of a slave for a capital offense. Any free Negro or Indian, being a Christian, shall be admitted as a witness, against or between any other Negroes or Indians, slave or free.

[3]Time increased to thirty days by 1792, Chap. 41.

Section 20. Thirty lashes are ordered for the Negro or Indian, bond or free, who shall lift his hand in opposition to any Christian, not being an Indian or Negro.

Section 21. It is still lawful to kill and destroy any outlying Negro by any ways or means without accusation or impeachment of any crime. For slaves killed in dispersing unlawful assemblies, pursuit of rebels, etc., a suitable allowance may be made the owners by the Assembly.

Section 22. An accidental homicide during correction of a slave still does not make one liable for prosecution or punishment, unless the slave is killed wilfully; on a manslaughter verdict, there is no forfeiture or punishment.

1748. Chapter XLI. The punishment for hogstealing by persons not slaves is, for the first offense, twenty-five lashes, well laid on; for the second offense, the pillory two hours and also ears nailed thereto; slaves, thirty-nine lashes; second conviction, two hours in pillory with ears nailed as before directed. No jury is necessary and the confession of the accused may be received, or the oath of one or more credible witnesses, or such testimony of Negroes or Indians, bond or free, as shall seem convincing. For third offense of hogstealing, every offender is a felon and shall suffer death without benefit of clergy.

1752. Chapter XLII. An act for preserving the breed of sheep here makes it unlawful for any Negro or slave to carry any dog in certain counties in going from one plantation to another, under penalty of twenty lashes on the bare back, except that persons are not to be hindered in sending their slaves from place to place with hounds, spaniels, pointing or setting dogs.

1753. Chapter VII. Section 12 states where free persons are punished by fines, servants shall be whipped, but no servant shall receive more than forty lashes at one time.

1765. Chapter XXVI. Special commissions of oyer and terminer gotten from the governor proving expensive and troublesome, the power of trying slaves is vested in justices without such particular commissions if they have such general powers given them when they are first commissioned.

When manslaughter is committed by a slave the offender shall be allowed benefit of clergy.

1769. Chapter XIX. An act to amend the law for the better government of servants and slaves says, that whereas dismembering is often disproportionate to the offense, and contrary to the principles of humanity, it shall not now be lawful to direct castration of any slave, except on conviction of an attempt to ravish a white woman.

1772. Chapter IX. Slaves convicted of housebreaking in the night, without stealing goods, are not excluded from benefit of clergy, unless the breaking, in the case of a free man, would be burglary. Hereafter, sentence of death shall not be passed upon a slave unless four of the court, being a majority, shall concur.

Whereas, there has been doubt touching the method of proceeding against outlying slaves, it is now enacted that no justice of the peace shall issue a proclamation authorizing any person to kill such a slave unless it appear that such slave is outlying and doing mischief; if any slave shall hereafter be killed by virtue of any proclamation issued contrary to this act, the owner shall not be paid by the public.

1785. Chapter LXXVII.   No Negro or mulatto shall be a witness, except in actions against Negroes, or in civil pleas wherein Negroes shall be parties.

1786. Chapter LVIII.   Justices of every county shall be trial courts for slaves charged with treason or felony, which trials shall be by five at the least, without juries, and the verdict of the justices must be unanimous; provided that when the death sentence is passed that thirty days shall elapse in cases of conspiracy, insurrection, or rebellion. The value of the slave shall be paid by the public to the owner. One being detained in slavery, and suing for his freedom, shall be tried in the same manner as a free man. No person having an interest in a slave shall sit upon the trial of such a slave.

1788. Chapter XXXVII.   Several evil-disposed persons have stolen the children of black free persons and have disposed of them as slaves. It is enacted that whoever steals or sells a free person for a slave, knowing the person to be free, shall suffer death without benefit of clergy.[4]

1788. Chapter XXIII.   This law repeals the act which declared that if a slave happened to die during correction by his owner, or by reason of any accidental blow, no person concerned in such correction or accidental homicide was liable to prosecution or forfeiture.[5]

1789. Chapter XXII.   This act repeats that a female shall stand in the same respect to clergy as a male, and declares that

[4]Passed in January, 1788.
[5]Passed in November, 1788.

a slave shall in all cases receive the same judgment and stand in the same condition with respect to the benefit of clergy as a free Negro or mulatto.

1790. Chapter LXIV. The mayor, recorder and aldermen of Richmond, or any five of them, may try slaves in the same manner as the justices of the county now do: Provided that their jurisdiction be limited to offenses committed within the jurisdiction of the Court of Hustings for the said city.

1792. Chapter 36. Any person not being a slave stealing a hog, for the first offense, shall receive on the bare back twenty-five lashes, well laid on, at the public whipping post, or pay thirty dollars to the county, and eight dollars for every hog; for a second offense, he shall stand two hours in the pillory and have both ears nailed for two hours.

If any servant is convicted of hogstealing, his owner shall pay eight dollars, whether it is for first or second offense, and shall be repaid for the same by the further service of the offender.

When slaves shall steal any hog, they shall be tried without jury, Negroes, bond or free, being permitted to testify, and if guilty they shall receive thirty-nine lashes for the first offense, and for the second offense, two hours in the pillory with ears nailed. If any Negro testify falsely, he shall receive the same corporal punishment as the slave tried for hogstealing.

Third offenders are felons.

1792. Chapter 41. No Negro or mulatto, bond or free, shall lift his hand in opposition to any person not being a Negro, under penalty of not exceeding thirty lashes on the bare back, well laid on, except when it shall appear that such Negro was wantonly assaulted and lifted his hand in self defense.

Slaves may not be castrated, except a slave who is convicted of an attempt to ravish a white woman.

The owner is not barred of his remedy when his slave is killed by any other person, or through the negligence of any surgeon, or other person undertaking the dismembering or cure of a slave so punished by court order.

If any person knowingly steal or sell any free person for a slave, he shall suffer death without benefit of clergy.

On trial of slaves a unanimous verdict is necessary and counsel is to be allowed, whose fee of five dollars shall be paid by the slave's owner.

The value of a slave condemned and executed, or dying before execution, shall be paid by the public to the owner.

Legal evidence against a slave is declared to be his confession, oath of one or more credible witnesses, or such testimony of Negroes, mulattoes, bond or free, with pregnant circumstances, as shall seem convincing.

If a Negro shall be convicted of an offense within the benefit of clergy, judgment of death shall not be given, but he shall be burnt in the hand in open court, and suffer such other corporal punishment as the court shall think fit.

If a Negro give false testimony, he shall without further trial have one ear nailed to the pillory for one hour and then the ear cut off and the other nailed and cut off in like manner, and moreover receive on his bare back thirty-nine lashes, well laid on, at the public whipping post, or such other punishment as the court shall think proper, not extending to life or limb.

1796. Chapter 2. The death penalty for all crimes, except murder in the first degree committed by free persons is abolished.⁵ Benefit of clergy is also forever abolished.

1798. Chapter 6. The punishment for stealing any Negro slave is made death until the penitentiary is ready and thereafter the punishment shall be three to eight years confinement.

1798. Chapter 23. This act places the same penalty on Negroes and mulattoes, bond or free, for hawking and peddling without a license as on other persons.

1801. Chapter 70. Any Negro, bond or free, shall be a good witness in pleas of the Commonwealth for or against Negroes, bond or free, or in civil pleas when free Negroes shall alone be parties.

1801. Chapter 71. It is a felony for any person to deliver any citizen of the Commonwealth or any other free person whomsoever to be transported; the punishment is set at one to ten years' confinement. Any person delivering or transporting another who shall be tried and executed for any criminal offense pretended to have been committed at any place whatsoever shall be adjudged a felon and suffer death.

1803. Chapter 4. High treason is a felony punishable by death; murder in the first and second degree is defined, etc., but this act does not extend to any slave.

---

⁵At the present time capital punishment is or may be used in cases of treason, murder in the first degree, robbery with violence, kidnapping with intent to extort money, rape, arson of a dwelling at night, burglary.

1805. Chapter 5. If any person shall steal any hog or pig, he shall be guilty of petty larceny and shall have the same punishment as in other cases of petty larceny.

If any slave shall hereafter attempt to ravish a white woman and shall be lawfully convicted, he shall be guilty of a felony.

1805. Chapter 48. The judgment for $100.00 rendered against Vincent Fortune upon his recognizance to appear as a witness against Wm. Scott, a Negro criminal, is remitted.

1808. Chapter 24. If any slave maliciously burn or set fire to a stable, cornhouse, or other house, or aid any slave, free Negro or mulatto to commit such an offense, he shall be guilty of a felony and suffer death, if the amount of the burning be to the value of $10.00.

If any slave burn any stack or cock of wheat or other grain or hay or advise or assist any other slave or free Negro so to do, he shall be burnt in the hand and receive on his back any number of lashes, not exceeding thirty-nine, as the court in its discretion may think fit to inflict.

1809. Chapter LII. Whereas, a Negro slave convicted of an attempt to commit rape was executed, the public treasury shall issue an order for $366.00 to the slave's owner, Samuel Kerfoot.

1814. Chapter LXXXIV. Two Negro slaves of Chesterfield County having been condemned to death for burglary, broke jail and have not since been heard from; the payment of $400.00 from the public treasury is authorized to Wm. Archer and Harry Heth, each respectively, owners of the said slaves.[7]

---

[7]Passed in November of this year.

1818. Chapter L.   No Negro, mulatto, or Indian, shall be admitted to give evidence but against or between Negroes, mulattoes, or Indians.[b]

1823. Chapter 34.   Certain trespasses are declared misdemeanors, punishable as at common law, but slaves shall be punished by stripes at the discretion of the court.

If any slave or free Negro shall attempt to ravish a white women, he, and his aiders and abettors, shall be adjudged guilty of felony and suffer death by hanging by the neck.

1828. Chapter 37.   If any slave shall hereafter commit simple larceny of a thing to the value of twenty dollars or less, he shall be tried by the justice of the peace, and punished by stripes, not exceeding thirty-nine.

1829. Chapter 22.   This chapter amends an act of 1818 and states that slaves burning stacks of wheat to the value of fifty dollars shall be deprived of benefit of clergy; slaves burning barns and so on not exceeding fifty dollars in value are to be allowed benefit of clergy; slaves receiving stolen goods shall be punished by stripes, not exceeding thirty-nine.

1835. Chapter 63.   Whereas, doubts have arisen whether slaves are bailable, it is enacted that slaves shall be let to bail who are apprehended for crimes not punishable with death or dismemberment, and if the crime be so punishable and only a light suspicion of guilt fall on the party, he shall be bailable. No slave shall be bailed after conviction of any felony.

---

[b]At the time of the Civil War a Negro or Indian was a competent witness in a case of the Commonwealth for or against a Negro or an Indian or in a civil case to which only Negroes or Indians were parties, but not in other cases.

1835. Chapter 65. Any free person who shall either in the day or night wilfully set fire to any woods, field, or grass, or anything capable of spreading fire, shall be guilty of a misdemeanor, and be liable also to civil action. If any slave shall commit the offense, he shall be guilty of felony but shall have the benefit of clergy. The remedy for negligently, though not wilfully, setting a fire and thereby injuring another shall be damages to the party aggrieved. Any slave committing such an offense shall be punished by stripes, not exceeding thirty-nine.

1835. Chapter 70. Driving any carryall, gig cart or other vehicle over any bridge faster than a walk is declared a wilful trespass with a penalty of five dollars for white or free colored persons, and ten lashes for a slave.

1836. Chapter 72. The punishment for disturbing or obstructing a railroad is not less than two nor more than five years, but if the guilty person is a slave, he shall suffer death without benefit of clergy.

1837. Chapter 71. Any slave or free Negro who shall ravish or attempt to ravish any white female person, infant or adult, shall be guilty of a felony and he and his abettors shall suffer death without benefit of clergy, any law, custom or usage to the contrary notwithstanding.

1837. Chapter 81. Oysters are not to be taken from certain waters between May 1 and October 1 and free white persons offending shall forfeit fifty dollars, and, moreover, if the conviction be on indictment, information or presentment, the defendant shall be imprisoned two months; free Negroes, twenty dollars, and in all cases of conviction, thirty-nine lashes; servants and slaves, thirty-nine lashes on the bare back, if not acting under direction of master or employer.

1838. Chapter 100.   Burning in the hand in any case whatsoever is abolished as a punishment for crime.

1839. Chapter 3.   This act, appropriating the public revenue, sets aside $12,000 for slaves executed and transported.[9]

1840. Chapter 61.   Slaves entitled to their freedom, after a term of years or after the death of another person, shall be tried as slaves.

1842. Chapter 84.   The day fixed for the meeting of the court for the trial of a slave charged with felony shall be not less than five nor more than ten days from the date of the warrant.

1848. Chapter 120.   The Criminal Code of this year reduces into one the several acts concerning crimes and punishment. By Chapter III of the Code, rape by a white person of a female over ten years of age forceably, or of a female under ten years of age, is punished by a penitentiary sentence of ten to twenty years. Abduction of a female with intent to defile, three to ten years. By Chapter VIII, if the same acts are committed by a free Negro, the punishment is death, or at the discretion of the jury confinement of five to twenty years.

Chapter IV, Section 20.   Any free person who shall steal a slave shall be punished by a confinement in the penitentiary two to ten years.[10]

---

[9]Each year an amount was appropriated for this purpose. In 1844 it was only $6,000, in 1858 and 1862, it was $35,000. See also 1864, Chapter 2, this chapter.
[10]This crime is classified as an offense against private property.

Section 22.   Fraudulently carrying a slave out of the state
without the master's consent: the punishment is two to ten
years, and the guilty person is liable to pay the owner double
the value of the slave.

Section 24.   Any skipper of any vessel sailing with a slave
on board without the consent of the owner, and any free person, traveling by land, who shall aid any slave to escape out
of this state, shall be considered as carrying off such a slave.

Section 25.   Any free person who shall advise a slave to abscond, or shall aid such slave to abscond by procuring him
a pass, or by furnishing him money, clothes, provisions or
other facilities, shall be confined in the penitentiary two to
five years.

Chapter X. Section 29.   Any person entitled to the possession of a slave who shall permit such slave to go at large,
trade as a free man or hire himself out, shall be fined $20.00
to $50.00, and such slave may be sold for the use of the Com-
monwealth.   ,

Section 30.   Permitting a slave of unsound mind, aged or
infirm to go at large without adequate support shall be punished by a fine of $20.00 to $50.00.

Sections 32–33.   Any free person who shall sell to a slave
any ardent spirits without consent in writing of the master
shall be fined not exceeding $50.00 for the first offense; sec-
ond offense, $100.00, and his license to sell spirits or to keep
an ordinary forfeited.

Any master or other person who shall give written permission to a slave whereby such slave shall obtain ardent spir-

its with intent that the same shall be sold or bartered for his own use shall be punished by not exceeding $50.00.

Section 38. Persons permitting slaves of others to remain on their plantations above four hours, without leave of the owner of the slave, shall be punished three dollars for each offense, and any person permitting five slaves to remain on his lot shall be fined one dollar for each slave, and such assembly of more than five slaves shall be an unlawful assembly.

Section 39. Every assemblage of slaves or free Negroes for religious worship, conducted by a slave or free Negro, and every such assemblage for the purpose of instruction in reading or writing by whomsoever conducted, and every such assemblage in the night time under whatsoever pretext shall be unlawful, and the punishment of any slave or free Negro not exceeding thirty-nine lashes.

Chapter XI. Section 22. Benefit of clergy is abolished.

Section 27. Criminal proceedings against Indians and persons of Indian descent shall be the same as against white persons.

Chapter XII.[11] Section 1. Any slave who shall commit any offense for the commission whereof a free person is punishable with death or confinement in the penitentiary for not less than three years shall be punished with death.

Sections 2, 3, 4, 5. Slaves shall be punishable by stripes, not exceeding thirty-nine at any one time; for offenses for the commission whereof a free person shall be confined less than three years. Such offenses if committed a second time shall be punished by death. Slaves also shall receive the death

---

[11]This material is under the headings, Offenses by Slaves and by Free Negroes.

penalty in cases of attempted rape of a white female, for conspiracy to rebel, or assault with intent to kill a white person.

Section 6, et seq. Slaves or free Negroes using provoking or menacing language or gestures to a white person, going from home without a pass, selling or preparing medicines, furnishing another slave with a pass, carrying fire arms, rioting or unlawfully assembling, are punishable by stripes, not exceding thirty-nine; also any slave or free Negro who shall preach or exhort or conduct any meeting for a religious or other purpose shall be punished by stripes, not exceeding thirty-nine.

Chapter XV. Section 21. If the offense be a felony and the party charged a slave or free Negro, except in the case of free Negroes charged with felonious homicide, or any offense punishable with death, the magistrate shall bail or commit him for trial at the next succeeding court.

Chapter XXVI. Section 1, et seq.[12] The county and corporation courts, consisting of five justices at the least, shall be courts of oyer and terminer, for the trial of slaves charged with any felony whatever, and of free Negroes charged with any felony, except homicide and where the punishment may be death. Such trial shall be without a jury, upon a charge entered of record and not by presentment, information or indictment.

Counsel shall be assigned any slave charged with felony.

No slave shall be condemned to death, nor free Negro condemned to the penitentiary unless all the trial justices agree.

---

[12]This material is under the heading Proceedings against Slaves, Free Negroes and Mulattoes.

The value of a slave condemned to death shall be paid to the owner by the Commonwealth.[13]

1852. Chapter 106. If a Negro play or bet at any game played with cards or dice, or bet on the sides of those who play at any such game, or if a white person play or bet with a Negro at any such game, such playing or betting, although not at a public place, and although there be not lost or won within twenty-four hours a greater sum, or anything of greater value, than $20.00, it shall be a misdemeanor.

1856. Chapter 51. It shall not be lawful for any druggist to sell to any free Negro, or to any slave any poisonous drug without the written permission of the owner or master.

1860. Chapter 31. Any person buying from or selling to a slave ardent spirits, without the written consent of his master, shall forfeit to the master four times the value of the thing sold, and also pay a fine of $20.00.

1864. Chapter 2. An appropriation to pay for slaves condemned and executed or reprieved for sale and transportation is made of $80,000.00, plus $2,000 to pay for the expenses of bringing condemned slaves to the penitentiary.[14]

1864. Chapter 63. In the case of a slave condemned to death, the governor may direct that the slave be sold at public auction and transported beyond the limits of the Confederate States. Bond shall be given by the purchaser that the slave shall never return into this state. In the case of a female slave convicted of any offense other than arson or a

---

[13]This was substantially the law in 1860; since 1819 counsel for the defense of a slave could be paid up to $25.00 by the owner.
[14]In 1861, Chapter 2, an extra appropriation of $10,000.00 was made for deficiencies in former appropriations for this purpose.

crime against a white person, which in the case of a free Negro would have been punishable with death, such female slave, and the children born after conviction may be sold unconditionally without bond.

1866. Chapter 17. All laws in respect to crimes and punishments, applicable to white persons, shall apply in like manner to colored persons and Indians unless otherwise especially provided.

All acts imposing on Negroes the penalty of stripes, where the same is not imposed on whites, are repealed; also chapters respecting offenses by Negroes.

1866. Chapter 24. Colored persons and Indians shall, if otherwise competent, and subject to the rules applicable to other persons, be admitted as witnesses in the following cases: in all civil proceedings, where a colored person or an Indian is a party; in all criminal proceedings in which a colored person or an Indian is a party, or in which the court is of the opinion that there is probable cause to believe that the offense was committed by a white person in conjunction with a colored person or Indian.

The testimony of colored persons shall in all cases be given ore tenus and not by deposition.

1867. Chapter 62. At the extra session it is enacted that hereafter colored persons shall be competent to testify in this state as if white.

1878. Chapter 311. If any person conspire with another to incite the colored population of the state to make insurrection, or to incite the white population to make insurrection against the colored population, he shall, whether such insurrection be made or not, be punished by confinement in the penitentiary five to ten years.[15]

1928. Chapter 213. The lynching of any person within the state by a mob is murder, and persons composing a mob which commits an assault and/or battery upon any person without authority of law shall be guilty of a felony.

---

[15]Still the law in Virginia.

CHAPTER VIII

The Development of Free Compulsory Education for Negroes and Whites

1631. Act VIII.   It is thought fit that upon every Sunday the minister shall half an hour or more before evening prayer examine and instruct the youth and ignorant persons of his parish in the ten commandments, the articles of belief, and in the Lord's prayer, and all fathers, mothers, masters and mistresses shall cause their children, servants and apprentices which have not learned the catechism to come to church, obediently to hear, and to be ordered by the minister until they have learned the same. If any parent, master, or mistress shall neglect this duty, he or she shall be censured by the courts.[1]

1642. Act XXXIV.   Orphans of divers deceased persons have been very much abused and prejudiced in their estates by the negligence of overseers and guardians of such orphans; it is therefore enacted that guardians and overseers shall carefully preserve the estates committed to their trust and render yearly accounts; they are enjoined to educate and instruct according to their best endeavors in the Christian religion and in the rudiments of learning and provide for them necessaries according to the competence of their estates.

1645. Act V.   It was enacted in 1641 that all ministers should preach in the forenoon and catechise in the afternoon of

---

[1] It was also in the same year ordered that ministers preach a sermon every Sunday, attend the sick and not give themselves to excess in drinking, or riot, spending their time idly by day or night, playing at dice, cards, or any other unlawful game.

every Sunday, and in case of failure to do so to forfeit 500
pounds of tobacco to be disposed of by the vestry for the use
parish; it is now further enacted that masters of families who
fail to send their children and servants to be instructed and
catechised by the minister shall suffer the like penalty that is
imposed on the minister.[2]

1646. Act XXVII. Whereas, sundry laws have been established by Parliament for the better education of youth in
honest and profitable trades and manufactures, as also to avoid
idleness wherewith such children are easily corrupted, or also
for the relief of poor parents, but as for the most part the
parents, either through fond indulgence, or perverse ob-
stinacy are most averse and unwilling to part with their children, it is enacted that the county commissioners at their discretion may make choice of two children in each county of
the age of eight or seven years at least, either male or female,
which are to be sent to James Citty to be employed in the
public flax houses in carding, knitting, spinning, etc. The
children are to be furnished with six barrels of corn, two
coverlets, or one rug and one blanket, one wooden bowl or
tray, two pewter spoons, a sow shote of six months old, two
laying hens, with convenient apparel, both linen and woolen,
with hose and shoes. For the better housing of the children,
two houses shall be built forty by sixty feet with eight foot
high pitch. It is further thought fit that the commissioners
have caution not to take up any children but from such parents who by reason of their poverty are disabled to maintain
and educate them.

---

[2] Passed at the second session.

1656. Act II. If an orphan's estate be so mean and inconsiderable that it will not reach a free education, then that orphan shall be bound to some manual trade till one and twenty years of age, except some friends or relations be willing to keep him with the increase of that small estate without diminution of the principal.[3]

1796. Chapter I. An act to establish public schools, passed December 22, states that it appears the great advantages which civilized and polished nations enjoy are principally derived from the invention and use of letters, and upon a review of the history of mankind it seems that, however favorable government founded on liberty, justice and order may be to human happiness, no permanency can be hoped for if the minds of the citizens are not rendered liberal and humane; so it is enacted that certain aldermen shall consider the expediency of establishing schools and at every one of these schools there shall be taught reading, writing and common arithmetic, and all the free children, male and female, shall be entitled to receive tuition gratis for the term of three years.

1805. Chapter 11. Paragraph five of an act to reduce into one the several acts concerning slaves, free Negroes and mulattoes declares that it shall not be lawful for the overseers of the poor who may hereafter bind out any black

---

[3]In 1670 an inquiry to Governor Berkeley, of Virginia, was submitted: What is the number of planters, servants and slaves in your plantation? The answer made in 1671 was: about 40,000 men, women and children of which there are 2,000 black slaves and 6,000 Christian servants, not above two or three ships of Negroes have come in seven years. What course is taken about instructing these people in the Christian religion? Answer: The same as in England but I thank God there are no free schools nor printing and I hope we shall not have them these hundred years. . . . God keep us from both.

In 1682 John Buckner was called before Lord Culpeper for printing the laws of 1680 without his excellency's license. Buckner and the printer were ordered to give a bond for one hundred pounds not to print anything thereafter until his majesty's pleasure should be known. Hening says that his majesty's pleasure was tardily communicated because the first evidence of printing thereafter in Virginia was the revised laws in the edition of 1733.

or mulatto orphan to require the master to teach such an orphan reading, writing or arithmetic.

1811. Chapter VIII. This act provides that as soon as a sufficient literary fund is provided, it shall be the duty of the directors to establish a school or schools for the education of the poor in each and every county of the Commonwealth.

1818. Chapter XI. School commissioners shall have the power to determine what number of poor children they shall educate, to authorize each of themselves to select so many poor children as they may deem expedient and to draw orders upon their treasurer for furnishing such children with books and materials for writing and ciphering. Poor children shall, with the assent of their father, or if no father, their mother, be sent to such school as convenient to be taught reading, writing, and arithmetic.

1829. Chapter 14. This act amending several acts concerning the Literary Fund declares that it shall be lawful for the school commissioners to appropriate not exceeding $100.00 a year for a good and sufficient teacher for any school house, provided that the inhabitants of the district shall raise by voluntary contribution an equal or greater sum for the same purpose; provided, also, that the school shall be a free school, for the instruction without fee or reward of every free white child within the district.

1831. Chapter XXXIX. All meetings of free Negroes or mulattoes at any school house, church, meeting house or other place for teaching them reading or writing, either in the day or the night shall be considered an unlawful assembly. Warrants shall direct any sworn officer to enter and disperse such Negroes and inflict corporal punishment on the offenders at the discretion of the justice, not exceeding twenty lashes. Any white person assembling to instruct free Negroes to read or write shall be fined not over $50.00, also be imprisoned not exceeding two months.

It is further enacted that if any white person for pay shall assemble with any slaves for the purpose of teaching them to read or write, he shall for each offense be fined, at the discretion of the justice, $10.00-$100.00.

1838.[4] Chapter 20. School commissioners are authorized to apply surplus revenue to colleges and academies within their counties as they deem advisable.

1840. Chapter 8. It shall be lawful for the overseers of the poor and the school commissioners to pay to the managers of the Female Orphan Asylum at Fredericksburg, Norfolk, Richmond, or other similar institutions for the support of education of poor girls, such amounts as they now are allowed to apply to the support and education of such poor girls within their counties.

1841. Chapter 22. The president and directors of the Literary Fund are hereby instructed to report to the next legislature a school system best adapted, in their opinion, to secure the benefits of education to the people of this Commonwealth.

1841. Chapter 23. The school commissioners of counties may allow such compensation for the tuition of poor school

---

[4]For penalty on free Negroes leaving the state to be educated in 1838, see Chapter V, ante 1838, Chap. 99.

children as the board shall authorize, not exceeding five cents for each day's school attendance of each child. No additional compensation shall be granted to any teacher who is not ascertained to possess a fair moral character and other proper qualifications for conducting a school of respectable grade.

1842. Chapter 224. Henry Juett Gray, of Rockingham County, a blind youth, is desirous of becoming a teacher of the blind, and it is necessary that he should have the services of a servant capable of reading and writing, which object cannot be permanently secured other than by the education of a young slave, Randolph, the property of said Henry Juett. It appears that the father of Henry Juett is willing to indemnify the public against any possible injury which might be apprehended from the misconduct of said slave; it is enacted that it shall be lawful for a competent white person to teach the said slave, Randolph, reading and writing without incurring the penalties of the law, but a bond must be given of not less than double the value of the slave at mature age, conditioned against any improper use by said slave of the art of reading and writing, and for the sale and removal of the said slave beyond the limits of this Commonwealth in the event of his conviction of any crime and provided also that the court of Rockingham County shall be satisfied that the said slave is a boy of good moral character and correct deportment.

1845. Chapter 26. Whereas, the welfare of all nations and the safety of free states are intimately connected with the general diffusion of education amongst the people, and, whereas, the experience of various countries demonstrates that those systems of public instruction are most efficient wherein the primary schools are supported at the common charge and freely open to all, it is enacted that in the County of Albemarle there shall be five commissioners to lay off districts, none to include more than forty square miles. In each district, at least one free school shall be established and maintained for not less than nine months a year to which all the white children, seven to eighteen years, shall be admitted free.[5]

1846. Chapter 40. It is said in this act that counties and cities shall lay off school districts and the commissioner of each district shall register all the children between five and sixteen years; he shall enter with any teacher any number of indigent children which the county or city quota will pay for at the rate of tuition allowed. There shall be a poll for taking the sense of the people on the question whether they desire to adopt a system of district free schools.

1846. Chapter 41. This act provides for the establishment of a district public school system after a poll of the people has been taken. When established all the white children, male and female, above six years of age shall be entitled to receive tuition free. Reading, writing and arithmetic shall be taught, and where practical English grammar, geography, history (especially of Virginia and the United States), the elements of physical sciences and such other and higher branches as the school commissioners direct.

1848. Criminal Code. Chapter 120. It is an unlawful assembly of slaves, free Negroes or mulattoes for the purpose

---

[5]There were similar acts for other counties.

of religious worship when such worship is conducted by a slave, free Negro, or mulatto, and every such assembly for the purpose of instruction in reading and writing, by whomsoever conducted, and every such assembly in the night time, under whatsoever pretext. For punishment, the slave or free Negro shall be seized and given stripes not exceeding thirty-nine.

Any white person assembling with slaves or free Negroes for purpose of instructing them to read or write, or associating with them in any unlawful assembly, shall be confined in jail not exceeding six months and fined not exceeding $100.00. Any such white person may be required to enter a recognizance with sufficient security to appear for trial, and in the meantime to keep the peace and be of good behavior.[6]

1866. Chapter 19. The master of any minor apprentice shall be bound to teach him reading, writing and arithmetic, whether it is expressly provided in the written agreement or not.

1867-1870. Constitution. Article VIII, Section 3. The General Assembly shall provide in its first session under this constitution a uniform system of public free schools, and for its gradual, equal, and full introduction into all counties of the state by 1876, or as much earlier as practical.

Section 4. The General Assembly shall have power to make such laws as shall not permit parents to allow their children to grow up in ignorance and vagrancy.

Section 8. The Assembly shall apply the annual interest on the Literary Fund, the capitation tax provided by this con-

---

[6]This is section 39 and 40 under offences against public policy. By the Code of 1860, whites could still be fined and jailed for teaching Negroes to read and write.

stitution for public free schools, and an annual tax upon the property of the state, for the equal benefit of all the people of the state, the number of children between five and twenty-one years in each district being the basis for the division.

Article X. Section 5. The Assembly may levy a tax not exceeding $1.00 per annum on every male citizen of twenty-one years, which shall be applied exclusively in aid of public free schools, and counties and cities may impose a capitation tax not exceeding 50 cents per annum for all purposes.

1870. Chapter 226. It is provided that every male person over twenty-one years not exempt from taxation for bodily infirmity shall be taxed $1.00 for public free school purposes.

1870. Chapter 259. This act provides for a system of free public schools for persons between five and twenty-one years, that white and colored persons shall not be taught in the same school but in separate schools, under the same general regulations as to management, usefulness and efficiency; and no person shall be allowed to attend whose father, not a pauper, has not paid the capitation tax in aid of schools.

1877. Chapter 38. The public schools shall be free to all persons between the ages of five and twenty-one years residing in the school district. Until 1880, persons between twenty-one and twenty-five years may be admitted on the prepayment of fees.

1877. Chapter 62. The appropriation to Hampton Normal and Agricultural Institute, Incorporated 1870, is made on condition that there be departments for instruction in agriculture, mechanic arts, military tactics. The governor is to appoint three of the six curators from persons of African descent, citizens of the Commonwealth.[7]

1884. Chapter 340. It is enacted that the president and faculty of the Virginia Normal and Collegiate Institute shall be required every year to conduct a normal course of instruction to continue for eight weeks for the benefit of the colored teachers in the public schools of the state, or those who expect to make teaching a profession.

1886. Chapter 44. The Colored Agricultural and Industrial Association of Virginia is incorporated for the purpose of annually holding a meeting at which the agricultural and industrial products of the colored people of this state may be exhibited, with a general office at Petersburg.

1887. Chapter 357. This act provides for a summer school in the Virginia Normal and Collegiate Institute for colored teachers for five weeks.

1902. Constitution. Article IX. Section 138. The Assembly may provide for the compulsory education of children between the ages of eight and twelve years, except such as are weak in body or mind, or can read and write, or are attending private schools, or are excused for cause by the district school trustees.

Section 140. White and colored children shall not be taught in the same school.

1906. Chapter 164. There shall be established an institution entitled The Virginia State School for Colored Deaf

---

[7]Previously, three of the five curators had been of African descent.

and Blind Children who cannot be educated in the ordinary schools of the state.

1908. Chapter 364. This act to provide, in certain cases, for the compulsory attendance of certain children upon schools, states that every parent or guardian having charge of any child between the ages of eight and twelve years shall be required to send such child to a public school for at least twelve weeks in each school year, at least six weeks of which shall be consecutive, unless the school trustees excuse the child for cause, or unless the child be weak in body or mind, can read and write, or is attending a private school, lives more than two miles from the nearest public school, or more than one mile from the line of an established public free school wagon route; provided, however, that this act shall not apply except and until the qualified voters of a county or city avail themselves of its provisions.

In places where the act shall be accepted a parent or guardian who fails to comply with the provisions of the act shall be fined $2.00 to $10.00 for the first offense, and $5.00 to $20.00 for subsequent offenses.

1908. Chapter 400. The public schools shall be free to all persons between the ages of seven and twenty years, provided that white and colored persons shall not be taught in the same school, tax payers of the state may send their children to any free school, although not resident therein, on certain conditions; attendance shall be in the district nearest the residence of pupils unless otherwise ordered by the district school board.

1914. Chapter 84. The schools of the state shall be free to any child six years of age, if in the opinion of the teacher and superintendent the child shall have reached a stage of maturity as to render it advisable to permit him to enter school.

1915. Chapter 139. School trustees may in their discretion admit as pupils persons between the ages of twenty and twenty-five years, on the pre-payment of fees. Pupils, regardless of age, may be admitted to night schools.

1918. Chapter 412. Children between the ages of eight and twelve years shall be sent to school for at least sixteen weeks in each school year; provided the act shall not apply in the case of any child weak in body or mind, able to read and write, etc.

1920. Chapter 70. Public school shall be free to all persons between the ages of seven and twenty years, residing within the district, (with certain regulations); persons six years of age may be admitted to primary grades, and persons under six years to kindergartens; provided that white and colored persons shall not be taught in the same school, but in separate schools, under the same general regulations as to management, usefulness and efficiency.

1922. Chapter 381. Every parent or guardian having control of a child who has reached his eighth birthday and has not passed the fourteenth shall send the child to school, but this shall not apply if the child has completed the elementary course of study, is lawfully employed, lives more than two miles from a school, unless transportation is provided within one mile of walking distance from the place the child lives, or is physically or mentally unfit, etc. Penalties for truancy are provided. Cities without adequate buildings are given two years to comply, but the time may be extended.

1928. Virginia Constitution, as revised. Section 138. The General Assembly may provide for the compulsory education of children of school age.

Section 140. White and colored children shall not be taught in the same school.

1928. Chapter 471. An efficient system of public schools of a minimum school term of 140 days shall be maintained in all the cities and counties of the state.

Section 682. The public schools shall be free to all persons between the ages of seven and twenty years residing within the county. Persons six years of age may be admitted to the primary grades and under six to kindergartens.

Section 683. A parent or guardian shall send every child who has reached his seventh birthday and has not passed his fifteenth to school, unless local boards change the age to from eight to sixteen years. Exceptions are made for children who are physically or mentally incapacitated for school work, suffering from contagious disease, have completed the elementary course of study and are actually and lawfully employed, live more than two miles from the school, unless transportation is provided within one mile of the place where the children live, etc.

Section 684. Parents failing to comply with this act shall be prosecuted.

Section 686. Where a child fails to go to school because the parent is unable to provide necessary clothes, the parent shall not be punished, unless the local school authorities furnish the child with necessary clothes paid for out of public funds.

Section 687. Any county or city without adequate buildings is allowed two years to make provision therefor, provided such time may be extended by the tax levying authorities.

1930. Chapter 412. An efficient system of a minimum school term of 160 days shall be established.

1930. Chapter 456. Every parent or guardian having control of any child who has reached his seventh birthday and has not passed the fifteenth shall send such a child to a public, private or denominational school or have him taught by a tutor approved by the superintendent. The act does not apply to children physically or mentally incapacitated for school work, nor to those suffering from contagious or infectious disease, nor to children who have completed the elementary course of study and are actually, regularly and lawfully employed, nor to children who live more than one and a half miles from a public school, unless public transportation is provided within one mile of the place where such children live.

It is required that every blind or partially blind, and every deaf child, six to eighteen years,[8] attend a school for the blind or the public schools, or a school for the deaf, for eight months, or during the scholastic year, unless the age is changed by the school board, and unless the child is elsewhere being taught or his condition renders instruction inexpedient or impractical.

---

[8] This age has since been changed to 7-15 years.

1936. Chapter 352. This law is designed to provide equal educational facilities for certain persons denied admission to Virginia state colleges, universities, and institutions of higher learning. It enacts that whenever any person bona fide resident and a citizen of this state, regardless of race and possessing the qualifications of health, character, ability and preparatory education customarily required for admission to any Virginia state college, or other state institution of higher learning, upon application is denied admission for any reason, by the board governing the institution, if it appear to the board's satisfaction that such person is unable to obtain from another Virginia state college or institution facilities equal to those applied for and that such equal educational facilities can be provided the applicant by a college or institution not operated as an agency of the state, whether such facilities are located in Virginia or elsewhere, the board so denying admission is hereby authorized, out of funds appropriated to such institution to pay to such person, or to the institution attended by him, as and when needed, such sum, if any, as may be necessary to supplement the amount which it would cost such person to attend the said state college or institution, so that such person will be enabled to secure such equal educational facilities elsewhere without additional cost . . . the board shall take into consideration tuition charges, living expenses and costs of transportation.

CHAPTER IX

War and the Negro

1723. Chapter II. Such free Negroes, mulattoes, or Indians as are capable may be listed and employed as drummers or trumpeters, upon invasion, insurrection, or rebellion; all such shall be obliged to attend and march with the militia, and do the duties of pioneers or such other servile labor as directed.[1]

1755. Chapter II. An act for regulating the militia requires free mulattoes, Negroes and Indians to appear without arms and be employed as drummers, trumpeters, or in such other servile labor as they shall be directed to perform.[2]

1757. Chapter III. All male persons under the age of sixty, imported servants excepted, shall be listed for the militia. Free Negroes shall appear and be employed as drummers, trumpeters, or pioneers or in any other servile labor.

1775. Chapter VII. An ordinance for punishing the enemies of America in this colony provides that white persons in arms against the colony are liable to imprisonment, their lands to be taken and cultivated, the profits to pay their debts and the balance to go to public use; provided the committee of safety may pardon them on their repentance. Slaves taken in arms, or in possession of the enemy through their own choice, shall be transported to any of the foreign West Indies

[1] By the law of 1705, "all male persons sixteen to sixty years" were liable to military duty.
[2] Passed at the August session.

and there sold and the money laid out in the purchase of arms and ammunition.

1777. Chapter I. It is declared that all free male persons, hired servants and apprentices, between sixteen and fifty years, shall be enrolled in the militia, except certain public officials, ministers of the Gospel, keepers of the public jail and hospital, millers, persons concerned in iron or lead work, etc. Free mulattoes shall be employed as drummers, fifers, or pioneers. Drums, fifes and colors shall be provided at public expense.

1777. Chapter II. This act provides for enlisting all able-bodied men above sixteen years, including apprentices and servants, except hired servants under written contract, etc., and also provides drafts to complete six new battalions. Whereas, several Negro slaves have deserted their masters, under pretense of being free men and have enlisted as soldiers, it is enacted that no recruiting officer shall enlist any Negro or mulatto until such Negro shall produce a certificate from a justice of the peace that he is a free man. '

1777. Chapter XXII. A certain John Barr, of Northumberland County, desired to free a Negro woman named Rachel and her child, also named Rachel, but the consent of the governor and council could not be procured because Lord Dunmore had withdrawn from the government; a codicil to the will of John Barr is here confirmed whereby he emancipated the said Rachels and gave to their sole use certain property.

1779. Chapter VI. It is enacted that every able-bodied free man who will enlist among the troops of this Commonwealth shall receive so much money as with the continental bounty shall make up seven hundred and fifty dollars, taking into account the bounty before paid, and the pay and rations allowed; he shall also be furnished with a coat, waistcoat, pair of overalls, two shirts, a pair of shoes, and a hat. At the end of the war the said soldiers, sailors and marines shall be entitled to a grant of one hundred acres of any unappropriated lands of this Commonwealth. Such as shall be disabled in the service, and the widows of those slain or dying shall be entitled to immediate relief and also to annual pensions. Officers and soldiers during service shall be exempt from taxation in their persons. Every recruiting officer shall from time to time give notice of the men enlisted to the governor. For every man who shall be reviewed by the officer appointed for that purpose the officer recruiting him shall receive $150.00, and when it shall become necessary to call for any greater number of regular troops than shall have been raised under this act, the number of those raised under this act shall be added to the number called for, and the quota of the aggregate number needed for each county settled. Every soldier who enlisted into the corps of volunteers commanded by Colonel George Rogers Clarke shall be entitled to a grant of two hundred acres of any unappropriated land, and for the better defense of this Commonwealth, it is enacted that four troops of horse shall be forthwith raised.[3]

1780. Chapters III and XII. Acts for recruiting this state's quota of troops to serve in the continental army provide for the raising forthwith of able-bodied men by counties; in order to encourage enlistments, the sum of $12,000 shall be paid to each recruit for the war, $8,000 for three years, and

---

[3]Half pay for life was promised generals, field officers, captains, physicians and others; Chapter IV, 1779, also dealt with raising troops for the defense of the Commonwealth.

each recruit who shall continue to serve faithfully to the end
of the war shall receive a healthy sound Negro, between the
ages of ten and thirty years, or fifty pounds in gold or silver
at the option of the soldier, and moreover be entitled to three
hundred acres of land.

The commanding officer shall immediately proceed to
draft by fair and impartial lot, but substitutes may serve.

Whereas, it has been the practice of many tradesmen to
entice their apprentices to enlist as soldiers and to sell them
as substitutes for large sums of money, it is enacted that if
any tradesman or other person, if not an able-bodied man
under fifty years to whom an infant is bound, shall receive
any money for the enlistment of his apprentice, he shall forfeit double the value of the gratuity received; if he is an able-
bodied man under fifty years, he shall be deemed a soldier.

1780. Chapter XXIV. It is enacted that so many of the slaves
conveyed by John Harmer, of Great Britain, to George
Harmer, now a citizen of this Commonwealth, as were sold
under the act concerning escheats and forfeitures from British subjects, and purchased by the public, shall be vested on
January 10th in and restored to George Harmer, except a
Negro named Ned, who shall from the passing of this act
be vested in the said George Harmer.

1782. Chapter VIII. An act for the recovery of slaves, horses
and other property lost during the Revolution declares that
any one having such property in his possession shall return
it to the owner, and if the owner is not known, advertise in
the *Virginia Gazette.* Wandering slaves may be committed
to prison for three months unless the owners sooner appear.

1783. Chapter III. During the Revolutionary War, many slaves were enlisted by their owners as substitutes for free persons, and were represented to the recruiting officers as free, and afterward the owners, contrary to the principles of justice, have attempted to force the slaves to return to servitude. Because such slaves have contributed toward American liberty and independence they are all deemed free and may sue, in forma pauperis, and may recover damages if detained.

Aberdeen, a Negro slave who has labored a number of years in the public service at the lead mines, is also hereby emancipated.[4]

1811. Chapter LXXX. It is lawful for Hannah, a free woman of color, who was liberated by the will of her owner in 1809 and who is the daughter of Samuel George, also a free man of color who served as a marine during the Revolutionary War, to remain as a free person within the state and enjoy therein all the rights and privileges which other free persons of color enjoy.

1812. Chapter CXXXVI. Aaron Weaver, a man of color, who served in the navy during the Revolutionary War and received two dangerous wounds in an engagement at the mouth of the York River, is allowed $50.00 for his present relief and is placed on the list of pensioners with an allowance of $50.00 per annum during life.

1814. Chapter IX. Depositions are to be received in courts of the carrying away or enticing away of slaves by the enemy, and the depositions sent to the executive of the state to be preserved among the archives of the state.

---

[4]Passed at the October session.

On the approach of any part of the enemy's naval force, the officers of the militia to prevent the desertion of slaves shall remove any boat which might be useful to a slave in deserting. Horses and men may be impressed to aid in the removal of any boat to a place of safety.

1814. XCII. A Negro man with a cart and horse was impressed last April in the service of the Commonwealth, and while in such service, the Negro, who before was a very valuable servant, received a fracture of the leg, which has rendered him entirely useless. John Dixon, of Gloucester County, the owner, is therefore allowed $350.00 damages.

1815. Chapter X. Doubts have arisen in the construction of an act regarding the desertion of slaves to the enemy; for explanation it is enacted that when there is probable cause to believe slaves disposed to desert to the enemy will attempt to use the boats of public ferries, a military guard to watch and protect the boats of the ferry shall be detailed; the guard to be paid as other militia in the service of the Commonwealth.[5]

1819. Chapter CLXIX. Whereas, it is represented to the General Assembly from the petition of James (alias James La Fayette) that during the Revolutionary War he was a slave, the property of William Armistead, of New Kent County, that he gained the consent of his master to join the services of the French under Lafayette, that in 1786 the services were considered so important that he was emancipated by the legislature and he is now poor; he is hereby authorized to receive $60.00 for his present relief, and $40.00 annually.[6]

[5]The war of 1812 ended in December, 1814, this act was passed January 6, 1815; probably the Assembly had not at this time heard the news.
[6]For acts on pensions, see 1779, IV; 1782, XXI; 1785, XLIV, etc.

1820. Chapter CXXXV. Richard Nicken, a free man of color, who enlisted for three years during the Revolutionary War and is now poor and infirm, is placed on the pension list for $60.00 annually and is to receive $50.00 for his present relief.

1821. Chapter 130. The sum of $60.00 is allowed George McCoy, a free man of color, of Rockingham County, who was a soldier of the Revolution and severely wounded and is now poor, old and infirm; he is also placed on the pension list for life.

1825. Chapter 32. Many citizens having sustained great loss by having their slaves and other property carried away by the enemy in the late war between England and the United States, thereby reducing a portion who enjoyed affluence to a state of poverty; it is enacted that certificates, affidavits and depositions necessary for prosecuting claims at Washington, shall be free from tax.

1826. Chapter 129. William Jones, a free man of color, a soldier of the Revolution from 1777-80, who is old and infirm, is placed on the pension list for $60.00 annually and shall receive $30.00 for his present relief.

1861. Chapter 85. The governor may employ all or any free Negroes sentenced to the penitentiary on public work, and cause them to be hired to the proprietor of iron works, manufacturing cannon or munitions of war, or any salt works, or any company manufacturing iron, or any internal improvement company.

Slaves sentenced to sale and transportation may be likewise employed.

1861. Ordinance No. 84. In July it is ordained that all able-bodied male free Negroes, between eighteen and fifty, shall be enrolled. They shall be selected as laborers, having reference to their condition and circumstances, and be entitled to such compensation, rations, quarters, and medical attendance as may be allowed other labor in the public service. Negroes who fail to obey when requisitioned shall be subject to the penalties provided for persons drafted from the militia who fail to obey.[7]

1862. Chapter 2. On October 3 it is enacted that the governor of the Commonwealth, when requested by the president of the Confederate States, is authorized to call into the service of the Confederate States for labor on fortifications and other works necessary for the public defense for a period not exceeding sixty days, a number of male slaves between eighteen and forty-five years, not exceeding ten thousand at any one time and not exceeding in any county or city five percentum of the entire slave population thereof. The sum of $16.00 per month for each slave shall be paid by the Confederate States to the holders of the slaves, and soldiers' rations, medicines, and medical attendance furnished; the value of such slaves as escape or are seized or killed by the public enemy shall be paid by the Confederate States to the owners of the slaves.

It shall be lawful for any number of persons who may be be required to furnish not less than thirty or more than forty slaves to place such slaves in charge of an agent or overseer selected by the owners, who shall deliver them to the Confederate States, and such overseer, if a fit and proper person,

---

[7]Ordinance No. 88 passed in 1861 provided for a draft from the State Militia for the Confederate Army.

shall be employed by the Confederate government in charge
of the slaves.

1862. Chapter 42. This is an act to amend and re-enact
an ordinance to provide for the enrollment and employment
of free Negroes in the public service, passed by Convention
July 1, 1861.

All able-bodied male free Negroes between the ages of
eighteen and fifty shall be enrolled. From the enrollment a
number of laborers, having reference to the condition and
circumstances of the parties, shall be selected. All such free
Negroes shall be entitled to compensation, rations, quarters
and medical attendance and shall not be detained longer
than one hundred and eighty days at any one time.

Free Negroes who fail to obey the requisition to appear
shall be subject to the penalties provided by law, for persons
drafted who fail to obey the draft.

Free Negroes may be accepted as volunteers. No requisition for labor shall be made until the free Negroes enrolled
according to this act shall be received into the public service.

1862. Chapter 43. This act authorizes the jails and poor
houses of the state to be used by the Confederate States for the
safekeeping of free Negroes arrested by military authority.

1862. Chapter 86. It is enacted that county courts of all
the tidewater counties shall have the power to adopt such
measures as in their opinion may be necessary to prevent the
escape of slaves in boats to the public enemy, and for this
purpose may remove all boats from the water, and when
necessary destroy them, the value to be paid the owners.

1862. Chapter 131. This act appropriates public money for jailers who have kept certain Negro convicts confined in the jail in the year 1861, the Negroes having been used on public works escaped from service and were apprehended as runaways.

1862. Resolution No. 9 of the Assembly on January 7 authorizes any number of free Negroes to be carried out of the state to be engaged in the manufacture of saltpetre and other munitions of war. At the expiration of the term for which the Negroes may hire themselves, liberty is reserved to them to return to Virginia.

1863. Chapter 6. On March 13 the military service age of slaves is changed to eighteen to fifty-five years and the monthly allowance to owners raised to $20.00. Any person who has lost one-third part of his slaves by the said slaves going over to the enemy is exempt from the operation of the law; also a widow having a son in service, or whose husband has died in service, owning only one slave, shall be exempt, etc. But no slave holder shall be exempt by reason of having slaves in the employment of the state or Confederate government.

1863. Chapter 34. This act authorizes the governor to hire the free Negro and slave convicts in the penitentiary to the owners of coal pits, also as many able-bodied white male convicts as can be spared from the penitentiary work shops, not exceeding one hundred and fifty.

1863. Resolution No. 4. The governor is authorized by this resolution of January 27 to suspend the act of October 3, 1862, to provide for the public defense in counties where

the loss of slaves by the presence of the public enemy has
been so great as to interfere with agriculture.

1864. Resolution No. 6. Whereas, the Congress of the Confederate States of America by act of February 13, 1864, for
the employment of free Negroes and slaves in certain ca-
pacities has declared that they shall be held liable to perform such duties with the army as the secretary of war may
prescribe, the governor is directed to request the secretary
of war to exempt certain Virginia counties in the possession
of the public enemy, or so threatened that any attempt to
remove the free Negroes would endanger their escape to the
public enemy.

1864. Resolution No. 13. Whereas, the recent requisition
by the Confederate authorities for slave labor to work on
fortifications will, if carried out, interfere seriously with the
farming production of the state, it is resolved that the governor of the state urge upon the authorities of the Confederate States the necessity of releasing slaves from requisition,
if in the judgment of the Confederate authorities, this re-
lease may be granted consistently with the necessities of the
military situation.

1928. Chapter 148. Any person who actually accompanied
a Confederate soldier in service and remained faithful
and loyal as a body servant, or who served as a cook, hos-
tler or teamster, or who worked on Confederate breast-
works, or who buried the Confederate dead, etc., shall be
entitled to receive an annual pension of $25.00.[8]

---

[8]Previous pension acts limited aid to citizens of Virginia disabled during the war
between the states while serving as soldiers, sailors, or marines, and certain widows.
See 1902, Chap. 453.

CHAPTER X

Abolition and Emancipation[1]

1776. Virginia Bill of Rights, passed June 12. I. All men are by nature equally free and independent and have certain inherent rights, namely, the enjoyment of life and liberty, with the means of acquiring and possessing property, and pursuing and obtaining happiness and safety.[2]

1778. Chapter I. Hereafter no slave shall be imported into the Commonwealth by sea or land.

1795. Chapter II. It is enacted that a person conceiving himself to be detained as a slave illegally may make complaint in court; the petitioner shall be assigned counsel.

1818. Chapter LI. Every poor person who has a cause of action against any person within the Commonwealth shall by the direction of the court before whom he would sue have writs without paying, counsel assigned, and costs remitted.

Slaves who conceive themselves illegally held may make complaint; the petitioner shall be assigned counsel.

If any person aid or abet a suit for freedom which is not established, on action he shall pay $100.00 to the owner of the slave.

[1] For acts dealing with individuals emancipated see chapters on Servants and Slaves, and Free Negroes. This chapter is intended to deal with the growth of the general principle of abolition and the emancipation movement as developed in legislative enactments, and the formal resolutions included in the official session laws.

[2] The principle here enunciated was readopted in later Virginia Constitutions. Note that the United States Constitution of 1789 stated: The migration or importation of such persons as any of the states think proper to admit, shall not be prohibited by the Congress prior to 1808, but a tax may be imposed on such importations, not exceeding $10.00 for each person. The slave trade was abolished in the United States, January 1, 1808.

In all cases, wherein the property of a person, held as a slave, demanding freedom shall come for trial, no person who is a member of any society for the emancipation of Negroes from the possession of their masters shall be admitted to serve as a juror.

1836. Chapter 66. An act to suppress the circulation of incendiary publications, and for other purposes, states: Whereas, attempts have recently been made by certain abolition or anti-slavery societies and evil-disposed persons, of some of the non-slave holding states to interfere with the relations existing between master and slave in this state and to excite in our colored population a spirit of insubordination, rebellion and insurrection, by distributing among them, through the United States mail and other means, certain incendiary books, or other writings of an inflammatory and mischievious tendency: To provide against the dangers thence arising, it is enacted, That members or agents of anti-slavery societies who shall come into this state and maintain that the owners of slaves have no property in them, or advocate or advise the abolition of slavery shall be guilty of a high misdemeanor, and shall suffer a fine $50.00 to $200.00 and imprisonment of six months to three years, at the discretion of the jury.

The penalty for writing or circulating any book advising or persuading to rebel, or denying the right of masters to property in their slaves shall be, if a slave or other colored person, not exceeding thirty-nine stripes, and transportation and sale beyond the United States; if a free white person, he shall be guilty of a felony with imprisonment of two to five years. Postmasters shall notify justices of the peace of the reception of such incendiary publications and it shall be the duty of the justice to have such books or other writings burned. If the person to whom the writing is directed subscribed for it, the justice shall commit him to jail. A penalty of $50.00 to $200.00 is set for the violation of the act by postmasters, one-half of the amount to go to the informer or any person who will sue for it, and one-half to the Literary Fund of the Commonwealth. Arrest of offenders who come into the state may be made by any free white person.

1836. Resolution No. 1. This resolution, relative to the interference of certain associations in the Northern States with domestic slavery in the South, states that this Commonwealth only has the right to control domestic slavery within its limits and will maintain this right at all hazards and calls on co-states to restrain and punish their citizens who form abolition societies. Furthermore, Congress has no power to abolish slavery in the District of Columbia or territories of the United States and any act having for its object the abolition of slavery therein would afford just cause of alarm to the slave-holding states and bring the Union into imminent peril.

1840. Resolution No. 1, relative to the refusal of the governor of New York to surrender three fugitives from justice who had feloniously stolen a Negro slave, now recovered, states that no private justice is delayed, therefore, nothing is involved but an important principle. The New York governor refused on the grounds that New York law did not recognize that one man could be the property of another or be stolen from another.

In a lengthy discussion of the legal and constitutional questions raised, Virginia maintains that by the universal

consent of all civilized nations one human being may be the
property of another; that every state, except Massachusetts,
at the adoption of the Constitution of the United States, admitted one man could be the property of another; that New
York only within a few years has abolished slavery. Virginia
statutes now in force were in force when the Federal Constitution was adopted and made the stealing of a slave a
felony; citizens of another state need not come into Virginia unless they choose; if they do come, they may violate
her laws and incur her penalties. If there was one feeling
more than any other which marked the conduct of Southern
men at the adoption of the Constitution, it was extreme jealousy and distrust of the Northern and Eastern sections of the
Union on the subject of slavery. The Southern States demanded that a clause be inserted providing for the capture
of fugitive slaves. Could the men who insisted on a provision
of that sort agree that the felon who should steal from a
master might go acquit? Such fatuity might be looked for
in madmen but not in statesmen.

There are bad men in every country who commit offenses
when they can profit by it. But what is still more probable, if
the course of the governor of New York is acquiesced in those
deluded enthusiasts of the North, who in pursuit of some thing
they know not what are spending thousands in efforts which
they must see, if they be not blinder than any one except a
fanatic, ever yet was, can never accomplish their effort, will
attempt to make those efforts practically efficient by coming
into our state and making it a labor of virtue to steal our
slaves and convey them to a more galling bondage than they
now suffer, in the Northern States.

Suppose one of those Northern fanatics, believing that the shedding of blood of wives and children of Southern slave-holders would be but an acceptable offering in the eyes of God, should come among us, and inciting our slaves to in-surrection should escape to New York; consistency would compel the governor of New York to refuse to deliver him on trial. He would say one man cannot be the property of another.

It is the pride and glory of our country to be an asylum for the persecuted and the oppressed of every nation, but should any state erect herself into a place of refuge for thieves and robbers, she would sully that glory. Virginia is prepared to make common cause with Georgia or any other slave-holding state. The patience of the South has already been too severely taxed; non-slave-holding states are warned that patience will be exhausted from repeated aggressions.

1841. Chapter 72. An act is here passed to prevent citi-zens of New York from carrying slaves out of this Common-wealth and to prevent the escape of persons charged with the commission of any crime, and requiring vessels to be in-spected before departure to New York. Certificates of inspec-tion are required that no slave or person held in service, or person charged with crime or taken on a vessel under penalty of $500.00; $1,000.00 bonds from New York owners of vessels are required to satisfy the owner of any slave carried away.

1841. Resolution No. 2 declares that it is the opinion of the Virginia Assembly that a fugitive legally charged with crime in New York, and demanded by the governor of that state, ought to be surrendered notwithstanding the refusal of the governor of New York so to act in a similar case.

1843. Chapter 88. Whenever the legislature of New York shall repeal its act entitled "an act to extend the right of trial by jury" passed 1840, and when the governor of New York shall moreover officially communicate to the executive of this state his willingness to surrender fugitives from justice from this state charged with the crime of stealing any slave from this Commonwealth, then the executive of this state is authorized to suspend by proclamation the operation of the Virginia act to prevent citizens of New York from carrying slaves out of this Commonwealth.

1844. Resolution No. 1. The General Assembly of Massachusetts is severely condemned by the General Assembly of Virginia because Massachusetts has suggested apportioning representation and taxation among the states according to their respective numbers of free persons. The General Assembly of Virginia cannot regard their resolution as in truth a proposition to amend the Federal Constitution, but virtually one to dissolve the Union.

1845. Chapter 72. This act amends the act of 1841 designed to prevent citizens of New York carrying away slaves and provides for the appointment by the governor of Virginia of official inspectors as may be expedient at or near the mouths of rivers of the Commonwealth which empty into the Atlantic Ocean.

1846. Chapter 96. The act to prevent citizens of New York from carrying away Virginia slaves and all amendments is repealed, except as to Accomac County.

1847. Resolution No. 1. Whereas, the House of Representatives of the United States has said, in appropriating money for the war with Mexico that slavery shall not exist in any territory acquired by the war, it is resolved that the government of the United States has no control directly, or indirectly, mediately or immediately, over the institution of slavery, and that in taking any such control, it transcends the limits of its legislative functions.

Resolved, that if in disregard of the Missouri Compromise and of every consideration of justice, of constitutional right and fraternal feeling, that fearful issue shall be forced upon the country which must result from the adoption of the proviso aforesaid, the people of Virginia can have no difficulty in choosing between the alternatives that will then remain of abject submission to aggression and outrage, or determined resistance on the other, at all hazards and to the last extremity.

Resolved, that the Assembly holds it to be the duty of every man in every section of this Confederacy, if the Union is dear to him, to oppose the passage of any law by which territory to be acquired may be subject to such a restriction.

Copies of this resolution are to be forwarded to the executives of the other states of the Union.

1849. Resolution No. 1. This resolution on the Wilmot Proviso and other kindred subjects, and in regard to slavery in the District of Columbia, repeats much of the resolution of the previous Assembly on the subject of federal interference with slavery, states that without the compromises in the constitution on slavery that the Union of states could never have been formed, that laws preventing the emigration of persons with their property are unconstitutional, and the passage of a law abolishing slavery or the slave trade in the

District of Columbia is a direct attack upon the institutions of the Southern States and to be resisted at every hazard.

1849. A resolution adopted on February 7 states that slave labor was comparatively worthless in the middle and Eastern States, that as early as March 1, 1780, Pennsylvania passed an act for the gradual abolition of slavery, followed in the same year by Massachusetts, and within a few years by all or nearly all the New England States; such was not the limited and precarious state of the institution of slavery in the Southern portion of this Confederacy. Its valuable agricultural staples had given full vigor to its growth and extension here. It already embraced one-third of the population of the Southern States and in Virginia exceeded thirty-nine per cent of her population. It had interwoven itself into all habits and feelings of our people; it had become an essential part of their social conditions: it formed their productive labor.

The resolution then reviews at length the contention that the Federal Constitution was adopted with slavery as its corner-stone, guaranteeing to slave-holding states the ownership of their slaves as property in every state to which they might escape. For many years after the adoption of the Constitution, the guaranty of the right to recapture fugitive slaves was held sacred by the people of the North; it is now painful to recur to the period when under the influence of sectional jealousy and political fanaticism those plighted engagements of public faith were ruthlessly cast aside.

The period alluded to is that when Missouri asked for admission to this confederacy. Missouri was admitted as a state free from any conditions that impaired her equality and sovereignty as a member of the confederacy.

To that extent the Constitution was saved from violence,
but the feeling engendered then has never slumbered. Irregular outbreaks of brutal violence and ferocity were only a
part of the machinery employed by the non-slave holders of
the North against their brethren of the South. Abolition societies were formed for the avowed purpose of protecting
fugitive slaves against recapture.

It is not to be expected that the people will submit to this
state of things. Unless some legal remedy be found, an illegal one will inevitably be resorted to. The territory of the
non-slave-holding states will be invaded by those who have
been robbed of their property, with the view to its capture.
But the disgrace of a petty border warfare may not be the
last or worst consequence. The glorious Union itself may be
rent asunder.

Look well at these solemn warnings and then at the actual
state of things. The condition of things is that at this day
very few of the owners of fugitive slaves have the hardihood
to pass the frontier of a non-slave-holding state and exercise
their undoubted, adjudicated, constitutional right of seizing
a fugitive. In such a condition this committee would be false
to their country, if they did not give utterance to their de-
liberate conviction that the continuance of this state of things
cannot be and ought not to be much longer endured by the
South, be the consequences what they may. The legislation
of the North providing jury trials* when a person is claimed
as a slave, defense of the slave at public cost, and liberty for
the slave if the jury finds in favor of the slave, aim insidious

---

*It is interesting to recall in this connection, the wording of the Bill of Rights in the
Virginia Constituton on the subject of juries: In controversies respecting property and
in suits between man and man, the ancient trial by jury is preferable to any other and
ought to be held sacred; adopted in 1776 end in successive Virginia Constitutions.

blows at the institution of slavery through the forms of honest legislation.

They are palpable frauds upon the South, calculated to excite her indignation and her contempt. Such laws give liberty to the Southern slave under the deceitful pretence of trial by jury.

But this class of laws has fallen far behind the spirit of the times and has yielded to a new brood of statutes, marked by deeper venom and more determined hostility. An act of Pennsylvania has gone a bowshot beyond all the rest in the legislative war against the constitutional rights of the slave-holding states. This law makes it penal to kidnap a free Negro, or to carry such Negro out of the state with the design of making him a slave. The Southern slave-holder, against whom the remaining sections of the act are directed, is passed upon by the legislature of this our sister state, along with kidnappers, thieves, felons. Such is the spirit of non-slave-holding legislation.

Our Northern brethren of this generation, for the most part, have forgotten or never knew that their ancestors received and that they are now enjoying a full equivalent for conceding to us the rights in question, or if they be well versed in the history of the compromises of 1788, it is feared they will seek to embarrass the recapture of slaves taking refuge in their borders because of their misguided and perverted sentiments of philanthropy and public policy.

It will, therefore, be difficult to legislate. We at least shall have discharged our duty by pointing out to that tribunal having cognizance of the subject, those remedies which may control and restrain the evil.

The committee recommends therefore that Congress amend the fugitive slave law of 1793 and confer on every commissioner, clerk and marshall of the federal courts, and every postmaster and collector of customs of the United States, the authority now granted to federal judges, to give to the claimant of a fugitive slave the certificate authorized, increase the penalty for obstructing a claimant from seizing his slave, and declare all assemblies for obstructing the process authorized by this act unlawful assemblies.

1850. Resolution No. 1. Whereas, the recent action of the General Assembly upon the Wilmot Proviso and kindred subjects in relation to fugitive slaves has met with violent denunciation and a systematic perseverance in the wrongs complained of in the non-slave-holding states and it is inevitable that the result of such a course of action on the part of a portion of the states must be to incite bitterness, destroy fraternal affection which have sustained our confederacy, and finally to dissolve the Union itself; it is resolved, that in the event of the passage of the Wilmot Proviso or any law abolishing the slave trade between the states, Virginia will be prepared to unite with her sister slave-holding states in convention or otherwise in the adoption of any measures necessary to provide for their mutual defense, or common safety.

1851. Resolution No. 1. Virginia deeply sympathizes with South Carolina in the feelings excited by the unwarrantable interference of certain of the non-slave-holding states with our common institutions, yet the legislature of Virginia deems it a duty to declare to South Carolina that the people of this state are unwilling to take any action in consequence of the same, calculated to destroy the integrity of the Union, declines to send delegates to a proposed Southern conference, and affectionately appeals to South Carolina to desist from any meditated secession. Virginia believes the Constitution of the United States, if faithfully administered, provides protection to all the states of the confederacy and all acts designed in any way injuriously to affect the institution of slavery deserve the most unqualified reprobation.

1850–1851. Constitution of Virginia on Slaves and Free Negroes: Slaves hereafter emancipated shall forfeit their freedom by remaining in the Commonwealth more than twelve months after they become actually free, and shall be reduced to slavery under such regulations as may be prescribed by law.

The General Assembly may impose such restrictions and conditions as they shall deem proper on the power of slave owners to emancipate their slaves; and may pass laws for the relief of the Commonwealth from the free Negro population, by removal or otherwise.

The General Assembly shall not emancipate any slave, or the descendant of any slave, either before or after the birth of such descendant.

1858. Chapter 10. This is an act to prevent and to punish the unlawful bridging of the Ohio River in manifest defiance of the authority of Virginia, which has repeatedly declined to authorize the erection of such a bridge; the exclusive proprietary right of this Commonwealth upon and in the said river and the soil under its waters having ever been asserted and maintained by Virginia.

1858. Resolution No. 35. This resolution commends the president of the United States for expressing in his recent message an opinion favorable to the admission of Kansas under the Lecompton constitution; Congress has no right to look further into the constitution submitted by Kansas, than to see that the said constitution is republican in form.

1859. Resolution No. 1. This is a resolution in which the Assembly declines to interpose to delay the execution of sentence of the court pronounced upon certain prisoners for crimes committed at Harpers Ferry.

1859. Resolution No. 2. A flag is accepted from certain patriotic citizens of Philadelphia, with an expression of their loyal devotion to the Union as framed and the Constitution as construed by the fathers of the republic. The Assembly gratefully accepts the gift as a renewed evidence of the patriotism of that heroic band of Northern conservatives who have long maintained an unequal conflict with the assailants of our rights and the enemies of our peace; wherever fate may impel us in the future, Virginia will cherish with affectionate gratitude the memory of those who so nobly defy the fury of fanaticism.

1859. Resolution No. 3. This resolution assures the representatives of the state in Congress of the warm sympathy of this General Assembly of Virginia in the struggle in which they are engaged, and recommends, in view of the public danger, the union of all the elements of opposition to black republicanism and its candidate for speaker, on any terms consistent with fairness and honor.

1860. Resolution No. 7. The payment of the expenses of the invasion of the state at Harpers Ferry is authorized with the following allowances: to non-commissioned officers and privates, the amount of three months' full pay; for those who served fifteen days, two months' pay; for those who served ten days, and to all others, one month's full pay.

1860. Resolution No. 18. It is directed that the board appointed to audit and pay the claims incident to the invasion of the state cause a uniform to be made and presented to the captain of the Jefferson Guards and to the privates of the company.⁴

1860. Resolution No. 31. This paper is adopted in response to the request of South Carolina and Mississippi for a conference of Southern States: The General Assembly recognizes an imperative necessity for decisive measures in our present relations with non-slave-holding states, but does not yet distrust the capacity of the Southern States by a wise and firm exercise of their reserved power to protect the rights and liberties of the people, and to preserve the Federal Union. We earnestly desire the concurrent action of the Southern States, but submit to South Carolina and Mississippi and all our sister states of the South that efficient co-operation will be more safely obtained by such direct legislative action of the several states, as may be necessary, than through the agency of an assemblage which can exercise no legitimate power, except to debate and advise.

1860. Chapter 425. This is an act to compensate Andrew Hunter, of Charlestown, in the amount of $1,500.00 for his legal services in prosecution against John Brown and others connected with the recent outrage at Harpers Ferry.

---

⁴This is in place of the bounty allowed other troops by the state.

1860. Chapter 439. Mrs. Bridget Boerley, whose husband was killed by someone of John Brown's party of insurgents at Harpers Ferry on October 17, 1859, shall be placed on the pension list and receive $96.00 for life, or as long as she remains a widow.

1860. Chapter 440–441. These sections allow pensions to men permanently disabled by gun shot wounds at Harpers Ferry.

1861. Chapter 3. This act for electing members of a convention provides for an election of delegates on February 4, 1861, and a separate poll, to take the sense of the qualified voters as to whether any action of the special convention dissolving our connections with the Federal Union or changing the organic law of the state, shall be submitted to the people.

1861. Resolution No. 1, passed January 8. The government of the Union has no power to declare war against any of the states, and when any one of the states shall determine under existing circumstances to withdraw from the Union, we are unalterably opposed to any attempt on the part of the federal government to coerce the same into reunion or re-submission and we will resist the same by all means in our power.[5]

---

[5] It may be well to consider this resolution and those following in this year, in the light of their national setting. The first guns of the Civil War were not fired at Fort Sumter until April 12, 1861, although in Charleston, South Carolina, a steamer trying to bring supplies to Fort Sumter had been fired on January 9, 1861, the day following Resolution No. 1. Lincoln called for volunteers to defend the Union on April 15, 1861, and Virginia voted on April 17, 1861, in a secret convention to withdraw its ratification to the United States Constitution. Lincoln had been elected in November, 1860, on a platform which denounced John Brown but pledged the shut-out of slavery from territories. On December 0, 1860, South Carolina had seceded. The Constitution of the Confederate States of America was adopted in February and March by representatives from Alabama, Florida, Georgia, Louisiana, Mississippi, South Carolina, and Texas. The seceded states seized government property within their boundaries.

1861. Resolution No. 2. On January 21 of this year it is resolved that if all efforts to reconcile the unhappy differences existing between the two sections of the country shall prove to be abortive, every consideration of honor and interest demands that Virginia shall unite her destiny with the slave-holding states of the South.

1861. Resolution No. 3. Other states, whether slave-holding or non-slave-holding, are invited to meet commissioners from Virginia to consider and if practical agree upon some suitable adjustment.

1861. Resolution No. 4. This resolution, adopted April 1, directs the governor of the Commonwealth to seize and detain for the use of the Commonwealth heavy guns made at Bellona foundry or arsenal near Richmond by the United States Government, and to that end order out the public guard, to arrest the contemplated removal of the guns beyond the reach of the state to Fortress Monroe, where they can only be needed for the purpose of intimidation and menace to Virginia.

1861. Ordinance No. 1. The people of Virginia do declare and ordain that the ratification of the Constitution of the United States is hereby repealed, and the union of Virginia and the other states under the aforesaid Constitution is hereby dissolved, to take affect when ratified by a majority of the votes of the people on the fourth Thursday in May, next; done in convention at Richmond, April 17, 1861.

1861. Ordinance No. 2. The convention entered into on April 24, 1861, between the commissioners of Virginia under the provisional government adopted by the Confederate States, is hereby ratified and confirmed; passed April 25.

1861. Ordinance No. 3. This ordinance of April 25 adopts the Constitution of the Confederate States, provided that the ordinance shall cease to have any legal effect if the people of the Commonwealth upon the vote directed to be taken on the ordinance of secession passed on April 17, 1861, shall reject the same.

1861. Ordinance No. 9. The governor of Virginia is authorized to call volunteers into the service of the state to repel invasion and protect the citizens of the state; passed April 17.

1861. Ordinance No. 11. The appointment of a commander of the military and naval forces of the state is provided for on April 19.

1861. Ordinance No. 43. County courts shall have the power to establish a regular police force, which shall be authorized to apprehend and carry forthwith before a justice of the peace any person whom they shall have just cause to suspect has violated any law of this state in regard to tampering with slaves.

1861. Resolution No. 1 of the special session at Wheeling.[6] Resolved by the General Assembly of Virginia that our senators and representatives be instructed to vote whatever supplies of men and money may be necessary to enable the Federal Government to maintain the supremacy of the laws, and

[6] For a better understanding of measures adopted by the Virginia Assembly at this period, certain measures adopted by the Wheeling Convention are included here.

preserve the integrity of the Union. They are also instructed to favor no compromise which does not contemplate the acknowledgment by all sections of the supremacy of the Constitution of the United States.

1861. Resolution No. 4 of the Wheeling Convention. General McClellan and his troops are thanked for the brilliant victories at Rich Mountain, Laurel Hill and Carrick's Ford.

1861. A Declaration of the People of Virginia, represented at Wheeling, June 13: The act of the General Assembly calling the convention which assembled at Richmond in February last, without the previously expressed consent of the majority of her people was a usurpation; the convention thus called has not only abused the power nominally entrusted to it, but with the connivance of the executive has usurped other powers to the injury of the people, which if permitted will inevitably subject them to a military despotism. It has been attempted to subvert the Union founded by Washington; it has attempted to transfer the allegiance of the people to an illegal confederacy of rebellion states, it has attempted to place the whole military force of the Commonwealth under the direction of such confederacy, for offensive as well as defensive purposes. It has instituted a reign of terror, making elections a mockery and a fraud, even before the passage of the pretended ordinance of secession, instituted war by seizure of the property of the Federal Government, and by organizing and mobilizing armies with the avowed purpose of capturing and destroying the Capitol of the Union, they have attempted to bring the allegiance of the people of the United States in direct conflict with their subordinate allegiance to a state. We, therefore, demand the reorganization of the government of the Commonwealth, and declare all acts of the Commonwealth tending to separate the Commonwealth from the United States void.[7]

1862. Chapter 6. Whereas, acts have been passed by the Congress of the United States authorizing the confiscation of the property and emancipation of the slaves of loyal and true citizens of Virginia and the Confederate States, it is enacted that any judge or commissioner acting under the authority of the United States or any of its laws who shall by any decision, subject to confiscation or sale the property of any citizen of this Commonwealth, and the purchasers of any such property, shall be jointly and severally liable for double the value of the property. The right of citizens to recover possession of such property is not jeopardized.

1862. Resolution No. 11. The convention at Wheeling on February 13 ratifies a proposed amendment to the Constitution of the United States, which would deny to Congress the power to abolish or interfere, within any state, with the domestic institutions thereof, including that of persons kept to labor.

1862. Resolution No. 28 of January 17 states that the public enemy, invited by domestic foes, are in power in some of counties of Virginia and are confiscating the property of loyal citizens, and otherwise oppressing them in a cruel manner, and, whereas, the traitors there, contemplating a division of

[7]The ordinances which follow provide for the reorganization of the state government, for the assembling of a state assembly at Wheeling which shall take oath to support the Constitution of the United States, notwithstanding the convention of Richmond of February 13th, 1861, the apprehending of all suspicious persons or citizens of any state at war with the United States, for the calling of the militia of the state to execute the laws of the Union, suppress insurrection and repel invasions, declaring null and void the proceedings of the Richmond convention of 1861, and providing for the formation of a new state out of a portion of Virginia, to be admitted into the Union of the states.

this time-honored Commonwealth have set up a pretended government, the legislature therefore resolves that in no event will the State of Virginia submit to the loss of a foot of her soil.

1862.   Resolution No. 13 of May 9 states that for more than a year the people of the North have waged a cruel, unjust, and unrelenting war against us. They deny us the inalienable right of self-government. Professing to be the peculiar friends of the black race, they have destroyed their peace and happiness, seducing them by false promises from the kind care of their hereditary owners, and having found them burdensome have cruelly cast them off by the thousands to starve and die.

It is resolved, as the solemn sense of the General Assembly of Virginia that the separation between the North and South is final and eternal, and whatsoever reverence for the Union may have lingered for a time in some minds, has been entirely dissipated by the cruel, rapacious, and atrocious conduct of our enemies.

1863.   Resolution No. 1.   On October 8, the Assembly says that since the passage of the resolution by the General Assembly in reference to the pretended separate government set up by domestic foes in some of the Virginia counties, and the resolution of the Assembly not to submit to a loss of a foot of soil, the government of the United States has attempted to form a new state out of the State of Virginia, and is upholding by the power of her armies, certain evil disposed and traitorous citizens of the state. Therefore, it is resolved that Virginia maintains fixed and unalterable the purpose and determination set forth by the last General Assembly.

1864. The Constitution of the State of Virginia, adopted at the Convention at Alexandria: Slavery is abolished and prohibited in the state forever; minors of African descent may be apprenticed on like conditions as white children, a capitation tax shall be levied on every white male inhabitant of twenty-one years, one-half of which shall be applied to education in free schools.

1864. Resolution No. 1.   This address to the soldiers of Virginia in the armies of the Confederate States is a lengthy exhortation reminding the soldiers that appeals for justice were spurned with contempt, and that this is a war to subjugate our sister states of the South commenced by Abraham Lincoln, forced upon us by the malice of a people whom we had not injured. Refined and virtuous women have been brutally insulted and manacled by soldiery, and have been led captive from their homes as hostages for Negroes. Under the hypocritical guise of liberating from slavery a population happier and more virtuous than themselves, they have sought to subject us to a yoke more galling than they have essayed to remove. An expedition had been projected to sack and fire the City of Richmond and consign its inhabitants to flames and death.

An avenging God suddenly summoned their atrocious leader from the scene of his wickedness, the name of Dahlgreen will be handed down to history as a fit associate in infamy with Butler, and a host of lesser criminals, who have disgraced humanity. Born to an inheritance of freedom, you cannot hesitate to choose between slavery and death, your lands will be divided among the banditti from the North and from Europe, who have invaded our state, a free Negro

population will be established in your midst, who will be
your social equals and military governors. Negro guards will,
at their pleasure, give you passes and safe conducts or arrest
you to be tried and punished by Negro magistrates, and to
these yourselves, your wives and children will be menial laborers and slaves. Such is the doom pronounced for the people of the South by the wicked race now warring upon us.
But we know it can never be executed. An army of veterans
has resolved that their country shall not be enslaved.

1865. Chapter XX. The session of the Virginia Assembly
convening at Alexandria ratifies the thirteenth amendment to
the Constitution of the United States abolishing slavery.

1865. Chapter VI. The Assembly in extra session at Richmond on June 22 says: The time has arrived when it would
be safe and expedient to restore the rights of voters, to certain persons. They must take the oath prescribed by the
amnesty proclamation of the President of the United States,
swearing to support the Constitution of the United States, and
to abide by the laws made during the rebellion, with reference to the emancipation of slaves, also an oath to uphold
and defend the government of Virginia restored by the convention at Wheeling, June 11, 1861.

1865. Joint Resolution, by the General Assembly at Richmond in extra session, June 23: The general policy of the
present federal administration and especially its policy in regard to reconstruction in Virginia is eminently wise, just and
proper, and merits the warm approval of the loyal people
of Virginia.

1866. Resolution No. 1. Resolved by the General Assembly of Virginia that the people of the Commonwealth cordially approve the policy pursued by Andrew Johnson, President of the United States, in the reorganization of the Union. We accept the result of the late contest and do not desire to renew what has been so conclusively determined. Involuntary service, except for crime, is abolished and ought not to be reestablished; the Negro race among us should be treated with justice, humanity and good faith.

1866. Chapter 17. The following acts are repealed: All acts relating to slaves and slavery, and free Negroes.

1867. Chapter 42. At the extra session it is enacted that the value of the service of a slave from the time of detention to emancipation shall be taken as the measure of damage, should the plaintiff recover in an action for the alleged conversion or detention of a slave.

1867–1870. Constitution of Virginia called in pursuance of an act of Congress of 1867. Bill of Rights; Sections 19 to 21: Slavery, except as punishment for crime, shall not exist in the state. All citizens of the state are declared to possess equal civil and political rights and public privileges.

The declaration of the political rights and privileges of the inhabitants of this state is hereby declared to be a part of the Constitution of this Commonwealth and shall not be violated on any pretense whatever.[8]

---

[8]These sections on slavery do not appear in the Constitution of 1902.

APPENDICES

APPENDIX I

THE STATUTES, CONSTITUTION, RESOLUTIONS AND ORDINANCES
QUOTED OR SUMMARIZED IN

BLACK LAWS OF VIRGINIA

ARRANGED BY CHAPTERS

CHAPTER I

1607-1630
1640
1642—Chap. XX
1645—Act II
1657—Act II
1657—Act XIV
1660-1661 ....XXIX, XII, XCIX
1662—Act VI
1662—Act VIII
1662—Act XII
1691—Act XI
1691—Act XVI
1696—Act I
1705—Act XLIX
1710—Chap. XII
1753—Chap. VII
1765—Chap. XXIV
1769—Chap. XXVII
1785—Chap. IV
1785—Chap. LX
1785—Chap. LXXVIII
1792—Chap. 40
1792—Chap. 41
1792—Chap. 42
1792—Chap. 72
1803—Chap. 6
1804—Chap. 15
1805—Chap. 11
1814—Chap. XCVIII
1818—Chap. XVIII
1833—Chap. 80
1833—Chap. 243
1848—Chap. 120
1853—Chap. 25
1866—Chap. 17
1866—Chap. 18
1867—Chap. 127

1867-1870—Constitution of Virginia
1873—Chap. 148
1875—Chap. 112
1878—Chap. 311
1879—Chap. 252
1910—Chap. 357
1924—Chap. 371
1930—Chap. 85
1932—Chap. 78

CHAPTER II

1623
1639—Act X
1642—Act XXI
1642—Act XXII
1642—Act XXVI
1642—Act XLI
1642—Act LX
1654—Act VI
1655—Act I
1657—Act XVIII
1657—Act XLVIII
1657—Act CXI
1657—Act CXIII
1658—Act III
1659—Act XIII
1660—Act XXII
1661—Act XV
1661—Act XCII
1661—Act CIII
1661—Act CIV
1661—Act CXXXVIII
1662—Act II
1663—Assembly Resolution
1663—Act VIII
1663—Act XVIII
1666—Act IX

APPENDICES

APPENDICES

CHAPTER V

APPENDICES

APPENDICES

APPENDICES

CHAPTER VIII

[231]

APPENDICES

APPENDIX II

The Foolish Priest John Ball

1381

"Of this imagination was a foolish priest in the county of Kent called John Ball, who, for his foolish words, had been three times in the archbishop of Canterbury's prison; for this priest used oftentimes, on the Sundays after mass, when the people were going out of the minster, to go into the cloister and preach, and made the people to assemble about him, and would say thus, 'Ah, ye good people, the matter goeth not well to pass in England, nor shall not do so till everything be common, and that there be no villains nor gentlemen, but that we may be all united together, and that the lords be no greater masters than we be. What have we deserved, or why should we be kept thus in serfdom? We be all come from one father and one mother, Adam and Eve; whereby can they say or show that they be greater lords than we be, saving by that they cause us to win and labor for what they dispend? They are clothed in velvet and camlet furred with grise, and we be vestured with poor cloth; they have their wines, spices, and good bread, and we have the drawing out of the chaff and drink water; they dwell in fair houses and we have the pain and travail, rain and wind in the fields; and by what cometh of our labors they keep and maintain their estates: we be called their bondmen, and without we do readily them service, we be beaten; and we have no sovereign to whom we may complain, nor that will hear us and do us right. Let us go to the king,—he is young,—and shew him what serfage we be in, and shew him how we will have it otherwise, or else we will provide us with some remedy, either by fairness or otherwise.' Thus John Ball said on Sundays, when the people issued out of the churches in the villages; wherefore many of the mean people loved him, and such as intended to no goodness said how he said truth; and so they would murmur one with another in the fields and in the ways as they went together, affirming how John Ball said truth."

—as told by Froissart.

APPENDIX III

PARTIAL LIST OF NATIONAL ORGANIZATIONS INTERESTED
IN NEGRO WELFARE PROBLEMS

Commission on Interracial Cooperation—Atlanta, Georgia.

National Urban League—New York City.

National Association for the Advancement of Colored People—New York
City.

Federal Council of Churches of Christ in America—Department of Race
Relations, New York City.

American Civil Liberties Union—New York City.

Rosenwald Fund—Chicago.

There are many other national organizations such as the Y. M. C. A.,
Y. W. C. A., National Recreation Association, etc., which have workers
or departments especially for Negro work. It is suggested that individuals
and groups needing advice on Negro welfare problems consult the organizations named, and also where organized, local councils of social agencies.
These councils sometimes maintain special subcouncils on Negro welfare
and make studies of Negro welfare problems. For instance, the Richmond
Council of Social Agencies conducted an intensive survey of Negro welfare problems in 1928-1929. This survey was directed and the report, "The
Negro in Richmond," was prepared by the present writer.

INDEX

INDEX

A

Abolition and the anti-slavery movement. See Emancipation, United States, Persons Mentioned by Name, etc.
  Advocating abolition a misdemeanor, 199
  Congress' rights on, 200, 227
  Fugitives and the altercation with New York, 200, 202, 203
  Fugitive slave law, 208
  Northern attitudes on, 200, 203, 204, 206, 207
  Writing or speaking on, 199, 200
Adultery, fornication, etc., 22, 23, 24, 25, 30, 32, 67
Agricultural products of colored people, 181
Alexandria, laws passed at, 218, 219
Allowances; amounts paid for Negroes, 52, 60, 79, 81, 86, 87, 88, 89, 91, 92, 93, 122, 152, 156, 158, 160, 162, 169, 192, 194, 220
Amendments to Federal Constitution, 71, 72, 142, 143, 219
American Colonization Society, 108
Apprentices, binding out, etc. See Introduction, 27, 29, 30, 38, 112, 116, 137, 174, 179, 188, 190
Appropriations
  Slaves executed or transported, 108, 165, 169
  Removal of free Negroes, 119
Ardent spirits. See Intoxicating liquors
Arms, ammunition. See Firearms
Arson, 163, 164
Assembly
  Who may be elected to, 127
  Elections for. See Elections

B

Bacon's laws, 45, 130
Baptism. See Christians, Slaves, etc.
Bastards and Bastardy, 21, 22, 23, 24, 26, 27, 28, 29, 30, 31, 33, 34, 58
Bellona Arsenal, 213
Benefit of Clergy, 52, 154, 155, 157, 158, 160, 161, 164, 167
Binding out. See Bastards, Apprentices, etc.
Bill of Rights, 198, 206, 220
Black Republicanism, 210
Boats, vessels, skippers, etc. See Vessels
Branding. See Slaves, Servants, Runaways, 37
Burial
  Public required, 40
  Burials and feasts, 45
Burning in the hand, 154, 160, 162, 165

C

Capital Punishment, 153, 157, 160, 161, 168
Capitation tax. See Taxes
Castration. See Dismemberment
Catechism, etc., to be taught, 172
Central Lunatic Asylum, 124
Children. See Apprentices, Bastards, Education, etc.
  Ages to be adjudged, 133
  Bond or free according to mother, 23, 50, 56
  Negro, Not tithable before twelve years, 130
  Of those voluntarily enslaved, 120, 121
  Poor to be educated, 175, 176
  Poor to be employed in flax houses, 173

INDEX

INDEX

INDEX

[245]

INDEX

Made in the USA
Middletown, DE
13 March 2017